Grow Your Own
TREE HUGGER

101 Activities to Teach Your Child How to Live Green

Wendy Rosenoff

Published by

krause publications

A subsidiary of F+W Media, Inc.

700 East State Street • Iola, WI 54990-0001
715-445-2214 • 888-457-2873
www.krausebooks.com

Our toll-free number to place an order or obtain
a free catalog is (800) 258-0929.

LOC: 2009923237
ISBN-13: 978-1-4402-0367-1
ISBN-10: 1-4402-0367-9

Designed by: Rachael Knier
Edited by: Candy Wiza
Photography by: Jon Rosenoff
Illustrations by: Rachael Knier

Printed in China

♻ **100% Recycled Paper**

Make the change to a sustainable lifestyle using expert advice and know-how garnered from our Simple Living books. We'll provide you with the knowledge to develop long-term self-sufficiency through traditional skills, energy-efficient technology and eco-friendly environmental applications with step-by-step instructions that will save you time and money.

Mission statement: *Enjoy the simple things in life while you reduce, reuse and recycle.*

Acknowledgments

Without photos, a book of this kind would just be a yawn, or possibly a drink coaster. A huge measure of gratitude goes to:

• Tony Iulo, for literally enlightening us in the world of studio photography. "Lighting up the lemon" was unknown territory for us and we thank you for your direction and friendship.

• Jim Cooper, for giving us the perfect setting to shoot everything from worms to Chinese dragons, sometimes during the early hours; we are more than appreciative.

Jon and Wendy

Dedication

For my children, Zachary, Hannah and Katrina, one of your big childhood memories is the van making sudden stops if there was interesting garbage at the curb. Our backyard was a continual tribute to extracting one more life out of large plastic toys that so often land curbside with plenty of fun left in them. Your bright faces and enthusiasm have always been my inspiration. Make your mark as caretakers of this earth and not just takers.

For my husband, Jon, whose action photography many have enjoyed. Suddenly, you were thrust into the world of light-boxes, backdrops, diffusers, composition and deadlines — you did it, and I thank you from the bottom of my heart!

For my parents, Hans and Ingrid, whose creative, gentle hands have designed everything from clothing and accessories to stage-sets, houses and lead-free steel strapping … and most importantly, lives.

I am grateful for these primary publications that have shaped my green worldview. Thank you for your continual commitment to sustainable living values and honest information.

www.grist.org
www.idealbite.com
www.motherjones.com
www.treehugger.com
www.utne.com

Wendy

*Make sustainable living choices as
second nature as brushing your teeth.*

Table of Contents

Introduction

Our lives are so rich and full that downtime has become a precious commodity. This book allows you to set aside just a small portion of time over the course of a year to grow a young person close to you into a tree hugger. Sustainable living is not just about loving trees around you, but more about changing lifestyle habits — from thinking disposable ends at the curb, to habits that cultivate a worldview to remedy the health of our landlord. As tenants of this great earth, our violations have been many, and we should have been evicted by now! It's our chance to renew the contract and prevent foreclosure.

Each Chat Point provides an opportunity to discuss with the child the significance of the activity and the reasons for change. Mini-Chat Points are in a language geared to the youngest participants. Above and Beyond! sections are for taking the activity a step further and digging into Web sites that may expand your knowledge base. Whether you do activities sequentially or jump from The Kitchen Sink to The Lab Report and dabble in The Studio Gallery in between, keep track of your progress using the illustrations at the end of each section. Perfection is not the goal, but rather the act of doing together, and the end result of a commitment to sustainable living goals.

It is my hope that each Chat Point will find a home in someone's life and become as commonplace as buckling your seat belt. Once upon a time that wasn't a habit either, now, it's the law!

Activities have noted Web sites for purchasing ingredients and/or materials used in the projects. The sites are listed for your convenience and are recommendations only. Please shop locally whenever possible.

Getting Started

To keep the sustainability factor alive from start to finish, all edible ingredients listed are suggested to be organic. Items listed under the Materials list ideally should come from the recycling bin or existent stash of supplies. Once existing arts and crafts supplies are exhausted, check out **www.ecosmartworld.com** for recyclable, easily refillable, non-toxic markers made from recycled materials. Give them as teacher gifts to launch even more sustainable teaching moments, possibly with roles reversed. While a hot glue gun is used in several activities, the best craft glue with eco ingredients is from **www.ecoglue.com** and that glue is used for all other activities. Any indication of markers can be interchanged with crayons, depending on the age of the participant. When it comes to ingredients and materials, be a label reader and choose the least chemically inclined products.

Four activities involve naturally derived colors:
• Musically Inclined
• Paint the Town Green
• Save the Polar Bears
• Tie-dye — Give It a Try

Below is the color key for use with these activities. Each food item should be boiled in the smallest amount of water possible without burning, chopped when appropriate, and in just enough water to cover. Allow to sit for at least 10 minutes to extract the natural pigments. Cool to room temperature before using. Making the colors is half the fun!

Color Key:
• Brown onion skins = orange, sometimes can achieve a deep red
• Red onion skins = burgundy
• Beets = pink
• Instant coffee = brown
• Curry = yellow
• Spinach leaves = light green
• Red cabbage = blue
• Pomegranate seeds = red

Section 1: The Lab Report
(science projects)

There are no safety goggles necessary in this green lab. A vision toward sustainable principles is the goal through insightful experiments and activities. Discover which window in your home or school is welcoming the most pollution. Be amazed at how quickly mold grows on organic produce, as nature intended, and how alarming to find the shelf life of conventional produce extending well beyond nature's clock when chemical preservatives get involved. Be a light (compact fluorescent or solar!) and share your results.

Bee a Finalist

monos
inosin
tetrasoc
pyropho

tartrazine

• Spelling bee chemistry •

Materials

Junk food packaging
Recycled notecards
Pencil or computer
Microphone from a game or a singer among you
Selection of healthy snack foods
Friends or family

Directions

1. Find 25 difficult-to-pronounce, ugly looking words on the ingredients list of the junk food packaging (keep packaging for reference).

2. Print the words on the notecards.

3. Begin by calling out each word for a different speller in rotation.

4. Once a winner is determined, try to figure out which junk foods have which ingredients.

5. Repeat the spelling bee with the same words to see if anyone does any better.

6. Conclude with healthy snack foods which have ingredients on the label that can be pronounced and understood.

dium
te
um
phate

polysorbate

Chat Point

Notice how short the natural food snacks ingredients are compared to the processed junk food ingredients. There likely will be words that you may not know on the healthy snacks, so look them up. Understand what you are eating and make good choices.

Mini-Chat Point

Labels are meant for reading. If you start doing that when you're little, you'll always be looking for the mysterious new ingredient that may not sound like it's food.

Above and Beyond!

Little label readers and young tree huggers eventually leave the nest. Keep informed and ahead by visiting **www.greenstudentu.com** for campus developments.

Better Than All the Rest

Sodium Lauryl Sulphate-Free Cleaner

skull & crossbones not included

• Happy lungs •

Materials

4 cups (960ml) white vinegar
½ cup (114g) baking soda
½ cup (120ml) lemon juice
Cleaned out spray bottle
Mixing bowl
Stirring spoon
Washable cleaning rag

Directions

1. Stir vinegar, baking soda and lemon juice together.

2. Pour into spray bottle.

3. Attack glass, furniture, floor and bathroom surfaces with washable cleaning rag.

Chat Point

Perhaps in the near future, the commonly heard quote, "I just bleached my bathroom" will be a thing of the past. Clean does not have a smell and the vinegar smell quickly dissipates after it has done the dirty work. The rash of cleaning product options available leads us to believe that we need a small artillery of chemicals to live a clean life. Scented or unscented, chemicals still smell of harshness.

Mini-Chat Point

You can help clean too. No skull and cross-bones to keep you from helping out in your own little way.

Above and Beyond!

Every cleaning chemical contaminates our land, water and air which is reason enough to eliminate a whole aisle in your grocery store circuit. When time does not allow for making your own homemade product, choose www.seventhgeneration.com for pure cleaning products of every kind in the U.S., Canada and the U.K.

Compounding Effect

• *Increasing in strength* •

Materials

Handful of worms from composter
 (field trip for the worms)
Leaf
Stuffed, porcelain, wooden or paper bird
Stuffed, porcelain, wooden or paper fox
3 apples
Knife for coring
3 feet (91cm) of twine
Scissors
4-foot (122cm) table

Directions

1. Place twine across the table.

2. Core apples with knife.

3. Take a mini-bite out of the first apple and string the apple onto the left side of the twine.

4. Take a normal-size bite of the next apple and string that apple onto the middle of the twine.

5. Finally, take two big bites out of the last apple and string the apple onto the right side of the twine.

6. Working from right to left, place the fox behind the apple with the largest bites.

7. Place the bird behind the middle apple.

8. Lastly, collect a few worms from the composter and place them on a leaf behind the apple on the left with the mini-bite.

9. Your display is complete and it's time to share the Chat Point with a friend.

Chat Point

Toxins in the environment compound as they work their way up the food chain. They accumulate in greater measure as one animal feeds on another. This demonstration has a short food chain as the fox does not have any natural predators. You can try longer food chains too.

Mini-Chat Point

Everything is connected, from the smallest animal who may eat something a wee bit poisonous to the next animal in the food chain who eats that animal and winds up having a wee bit more something poisonous. It's like the snowball you roll, starting out the size of your hands and ending up the size of you. This is why we have to start at the bottom of the food chain, making sure our grass is free of poisons so that the worms will be free of poison, so that the robin will be free of poison, so that the fox will be free of poison. It works for humans too!

Above and Beyond!

By eating low on the food chain, the chemical load is reduced. Think of a four-month-old sardine versus a nine-year-old swordfish or a 40-year-old tuna. Fruits, vegetables and nuts without pesticide residue are the ultimate chemical load busters. Visit **www.veg.ca** and enter "eat low on the food chain" and read everything from this site that highlights these words — grab some tea, this site has an abundant amount of information.

Delegation of Pest Control Duties

PEST·IC
FREE ZONE

Materials

Time to go to a local garden nursery or visit an online source

Purchased ladybugs and/or praying mantis egg sacs

Garden area for release

Willingness to follow complete directions for care of ladybugs and praying mantes until release date

Directions

1. For releasing ladybugs into a garden, plan a gathering of friends and family.

2. Research the natural pest-control abilities of the ladybug and be ready to share facts.

3. Take care of the praying mantes' sacs and be ready to accommodate and feed several hundred wee ones when they hatch.

4. Upon maturity, schedule another garden release with friends and family as the fascinating praying mantis is not a sight to keep to oneself.

5. Research what a praying mantis will do as a caretaker in the garden and share facts.

Chat Point

Ladybugs are simple, natural and beautiful additions to the garden dynamic. They manage the populations of aphids, leafhoppers and more. The praying mantes are impressive from sac to maturity and will feed on all manner of bugs that would otherwise be eating holes in your greenery.

Mini-Chat Point

"A ladybug landed on me!" is always a thrill. A praying mantis landing on you may be a little more intense, but it's also a thrill. Both of these insects work to keep down the population of other bugs so that they don't destroy plants.

Above and Beyond!

If your garden nursery does not stock natural pest controls, ask them to visit **www.beyondpesticides.org** to learn more. Then, post a sign in your garden or lawn to show a pesticide-free zone.

Epidermis Squirmis

No More Epidermis Squirmis

• Skin — The window to your body •

Materials

2 tablespoons (30ml) olive oil
2 tablespoons (30ml) coconut oil (similar to solid
  vegetable shortening)
2 drops essential oil of choice (**www.auracacia.com**)
Ramekin or clean, recycled container with or without lid
Small pan

Directions

1. Over low heat, melt coconut oil into a liquid.

2. Turn off heat and add olive oil.

3. Stir in essential oil of choice. (I like lavender, orange or vanilla.)

4. Pour into container and allow one hour to solidify.

5. Use as you would any moisturizer.

6. Make in small amounts to maximize freshness factor.

Chat Point

Would you rather kiss someone with (a) coconut oil, or (b) petroleum on his or her lips? Your skin is the largest window into your body. What gets absorbed should be as pure and organic as possible and something you can pronounce. Propylene glycol does not sound like something you would want to rub on your skin but it is in many moisturizers and lotions. It is also commonly used in anti-freeze and brake fluid where it is noted as a dangerous chemical in a larger quantity. Much of what goes into skin care products requires synthetic fragrances to mask the odor of petroleum-based products. Why not combine a few natural ingredients and then you will know what is in your potion. Less is more, whether it is the ingredient list or the number of toiletries that settle onto our home shelves.

Mini-Chat Point

Since you don't know what the mad scientists have put in your creams and lotions, especially under fragrances where they are allowed to hide their secrets, making your own is more fun and better for your skin.

Above and Beyond!

Look into **www.thegreenguide.com** and search for "the dirty dozen" of skin offenses. If your local health food or grocery store does not have organic olive oil or coconut oil, visit **www.spectrumorganics.com** and **www.nutiva.com**. Watch out for those petroleum lips too.

19

Essential Potion

organic

panic

remover

• Organic panic remover •

Materials

20-ounce (600ml) soda bottle rescued from recycling bin, cleaned and label removed
2 cups (480ml) filtered or purified water
1¼ cups (284g) baking soda
1¼ cups (284g) Epsom salt
1 cup (227g) dried milk powder
½ cup (114g) citric acid powder (available at most health foods stores)
5 drops of essential oil such as grapefruit, lavender or orange (www.auracacia.com)
Funnel or rolled paper cone
Hand-held whisk
Decorative ribbon
Paper and markers or printed label from the computer
Alternative lid, if available, from another bottle of similar size to give the potion a new twist
Glue

Directions

1. Whisk together baking soda, Epsom salt, dried milk, water and citric acid until lump-free.

2. Add essential oil, adjusting for personal preference of scent strength.

3. Use funnel or rolled paper cone to pour bath potion into bottle.

4. Add water to fill.

5. Place cap or alternative lid on bottle and wipe dry.

6. Create an interesting label with noted name and make date and glue on bottle front.

7. Trim by gluing ribbon in place.

8. Make more to give away as a sustainable home spa treatment gift.

9. To use, pour one third of mix into bath under running water.

Chat Point

While a short shower with a low-flow shower head is optimal, sometimes a full drawn bath is inexpensive therapy for physical and emotional stress relief. Use organic ingredients (even dried milk powder is available in organic form) to make the purest addition to your bath water. Adding conventional bath products that include fragrance and color chemicals detracts from the therapy session.

Mini-Chat Point

Find new pleasure and learning in the bathtub by enjoying products from www.perennialtoys.com, including a narwhal and floating iceberg made from phthalate-free plastic, arctic animals poster printed on hemp paper, King Eider phthalate-free duck, and more.

Above and Beyond!

Try a bath-water filter from www.gaiam.com to help protect you from marinating in a bathtub full of impurities.

Life Without Bees

• Colony collapse disorder revolution •

Materials

1 bee representative from your existing toy collection;
  even a marble with bee colors
6 choices of fruits, vegetables and nuts
4 empty cereal boxes
Circular background object such as a Frisbee®,
  painter's color wheel or a snow disc
Hot glue gun
Scissors
Ruler

Directions

1. Plug in glue gun to preheat.

2. Cut flat panels out of cereal boxes, resulting in eight panels (one extra for mistakes).

3. Using a ruler, draw a hexagon shape of the same dimension on each of the seven flat cereal-box panels.

4. Measure 1" (25mm) inward from the hexagon shape outline and mark with dotted lines to form an inner hexagon shape.

5. Cut out the seven hexagon cells on the outer ruler lines.

6. On each hexagon cell, make small triangular snips in each corner down to the dotted line to allow for bending the cell walls on each side.

7. To shape the cells, fold cardboard back and forth on the dotted lines to form the cell walls.

8. Using the glue gun, join hexagons around one central hexagon.

9. Glue completed cell hexagon onto circular background object.

10. Leaving center cell for honeybee, glue fruits, vegetables and nuts onto surrounding cells.

Chat Point

Unless you are a bear with a fondness for scooping honey out of unsuspecting bee-hives, you may not miss honey too much if it were gone forever. We have a whole world of sweeteners, healthy and unhealthy ones, but life without fruits, vegetables and nuts is a whole different picture. The humble honey-bee is the most important pollinator for crops. With the mystery of Colony Collapse Disorder still unsolved, we have to examine the sus-pected culprit — pesticide use — and support environmental principles that make their world possible so that ours can continue.

Mini-Chat Point

After making your own honeybee cells, serve fruits, vegetables and nuts in it at your next play-date (remove the glued objects and any glue residue). Tell a friend about what the honeybee does besides making honey.

Above and Beyond!

Visit **www.hollymosher.com** and scroll down to the documentary, the Vanishing of the Bees. Host a home movie night and spread awareness. Give a goodie bag of multi-purpose propolis salve from **www.honeygardens.com**.

Triclosan - Not a Fan

• Molecular beachfront properties •

Materials

Common antimicrobial liquid soap
Dr. Bronner's lavender liquid soap (or any similar soap)
Graph paper
Pencil or computer
Ruler
Highlighters

Directions

1. Create a two-column chart using graph paper.

2. Make a list of the active ingredients and inactive ingredients found in each soap product, keeping the ingredients in the correct column.

3. Turn the paper into the landscape position and draw a bar over each ingredient word.

4. Highlight each set of product ingredients with a different highlighter color.

5. Analyze your untraditional bar graph and look up terms from each column that you don't know.

Glycerin
Sodium Chloride
PEG-18 Glyceryl Oleate/Cocoate
Fragrance
Cocamide MEA
DMDM Hydantoin
Tetrasodium EDTA
Citric Acid
Yellow 5
Red 4

Water
Saponified Organic Coconut Oil*
Saponified Organic Olive Oil*
Organic Glycerin
Organic Cannabis Sativa (Hemp) Seed Oil
Organic Simmondsia Chinensis (Jojoba) Seed Oil
Organic Lavandula Angustifolia (Lavender) Oil
Lavandula Hybrida (Lavandin) Extract
Citric Acid
Tocopherol

Certified Fair Trade by IMO

Chat Point

Contemplate why it might be necessary to have so many chemicals take the place of ingredients like lavender with natural antiseptic properties. Antimicrobial soap's active ingredient is triclosan. It shows up in the blood (through testing) of most Americans and has been found on the beaches of Newfoundland, most U.S. waterways and in breast milk. Steer clear of products with triclosan in favor of plant-derived alternatives that you know are safe.

Mini-Chat Point

Who invited triclosan to the beach? It's just not OK!

Above and Beyond!

Go to **www.bodyburden.org**, look under Chemical and pick your poison. Learn about parabens, phthalates, and triclosan in detail. Visiting **www.eoproducts.com** will show you a useful and informative Green Glossary about personal care products in general.

End Sponging Off the Earth

• Sprouting up •

Materials

Old sponges
Sprouting seeds, such as alfalfa and watercress
Tray or plate with sides to hold small build-up of water
Scissors

Directions

1. Rinse sponges thoroughly with water, finishing with a boiling water rinse.

2. Cut sponges into the letters of your name or a fun word.

3. Set the sponges in place on the tray or plate.

4. Water sponges thoroughly, and then tip the tray or plate to drain the excess water.

5. Push sprouting seeds into the surface of the sponge and set on a windowsill.

6. Water the sponges every day, taking care not to wash the seeds off the sponge.

7. Drain excess water from the tray.

Chat Point

Learn how to sprout seeds on a regular basis. It's a great method to have continuous fresh salad greens with minimal effort.

Mini-Chat Point

Save enough sponges to grow all the letters of the alphabet — Wow!

Above and Beyond!

For the history, nutritional value and recipes for sprouts, go to **www.isga-sprouts.org**.

Invite Some Worms to Dinner

• Black gold •

Materials

Corner in yard
2 bales of straw for corner fence property or 4 bales of
  straw to form square
In-house container to collect food scraps for outdoor
  composting
Regular eating habits
Shovel

Directions

1. Find a corner where a composting site can be set up in the yard.

2. If a fenced corner is in the yard, the fence will form two sides and the two straw bales will box it into a square.

3. Find dimensions of actual compost area after setting the two or four straw bales in place.

4. Set straw bales aside.

5. Shovel the inner perimeter of the area to a depth of 6" (16cm), turning over the dirt until it is loose.

6. Return straw bales to their original position.

7. Set up a collection container under the sink in the kitchen for all food scraps, excluding meat and dairy.

8. Add your container contents and grass clippings from lawn mowing to the compost area.

9. Using shovel, turn over contents to mix with loose soil.

10. As weeks and months go by, the worm population should grow.

11. Continue to periodically turn over the pile.

12. Use bottom layers of rich fertile soil from composting for spring gardening needs.

Chat Point

While everyone's backyard and animal population differ, this open and easy style may not work for those with hungry critters. Types and styles of compost units are plentiful and covered to keep the worm environment whole. Apartments can accommodate under-the-sink worm bins with newspaper to start, as found on gardening Web sites.

Mini-Chat Point

Worms are the ultimate pets who don't bark or wake anyone up and they poop rich soil as a gift to your garden.

Above and Beyond

For more compost information and comprehensive tips, visit **www.compostguide.com** or check out *Your Eco-Friendly Yard* at **www.krausebooks.com**.

BUMMER

GREEN LABEL ORGANIC

earth...
I call it home

i love organics

• Wear a shirt story •

Materials

Organic cotton T-shirts with environmental messages
Friends or family members
Camera

Directions

1. Dress friends and family in organic cotton T-shirts.

2. Arrange the messages on the T-shirts to make a phrase, sentence or short story.

3. Take a picture and email to more friends.

Chat Point

Conventional cotton is one of the most pesticide-intensive crops taking a great toll on the earth. Support organic cotton growers and producers by choosing to buy pesticide-free products. Follow the trend of runner's clubs and marathon organizers who have set the wheels in motion with organic cotton and bamboo T-shirts.

Mini-Chat Point

You don't want to be an eco-bully. A shirt with a cool green message is a fabulous fashion statement!

Above and Beyond!

Finding a shirt on **www.greenlabel.com** will help you get the message out.

Operation Strawberry Fields

• You spin me right round •

Materials

Saved, scratched, unwanted CDs
Lengths of ribbon and string
Backyard or rooftop garden with berry bushes or
  plants

Directions

1. Tie ribbon and string through the CD centers, leaving a length for hanging in a bush or tree.

2. Find favorite berry bushes and liberally hang the CDs all around.

Chat Point

While birds are delightful and wanted in so many ways, the fine-feathered friends always seem to win the race to the just-ripened berry. The CDs will move in the wind and chase the birds away. Enjoy your harvest without berry theft.

Mini-Chat Point

We usually welcome birds with feeders and often cameras, but this is the one time we want to redirect them somewhere else. The CDs make colorful sun catchers too.

Above and Beyond!

When CDs are no longer wanted, inquire at the local library to see if they can use the CD cases. With all the borrowing going on, cases are easily and often broken. Not buying more than we really will use, listen to or consume is the starting point. View a 20-minute clip about "Stuff" at **www.storyofstuff.com**.

Organic vs. Conventional

The term organic is indicated at point of purchase with a standard specific to each region which excludes chemicals from the growing methods. Conventionally grown produce can include use of chemically based fertilizers, pesticides, fungicides and herbicides.

Materials

Available fruit or vegetable in organic and conventional versions
Available shelf or drawer space in the refrigerator
Permanent marker

Directions

1. Mark the fruit or vegetables of choice as organic and conventional.

2. Locate an appropriate spot in the refrigerator.

3. Be consistent in terms of air exposure, wrapped or unwrapped, bagged or not, etc.

4. As days pass, sneak a peek at the duo.

5. After several days, the organic fruit/vegetable should be looking quite green, even if it did not begin as a green produce item.

Chat Point

Real food without preservatives, gassing, irradiation or otherwise, breaks down and spoils as nature intended. Conventional produce has a scary shelf life in comparison and leads us to the topic of frankenfoods (now an expression used to refer to genetically modified organisms (GMOs) that researchers are developing for market use in some countries).

Mini-Chat Point

The two lemons in the picture may share the same birthday, but they are not cut from the same mold. The organic lemon is doing what a real lemon is supposed to do — get moldy. The conventional lemon looks like it was just picked off the tree — that's not real.

Above and Beyond!

For a GMO primer, visit **www.frankenfoods.com** and learn both sides of the story.

Positive Reactions

CORN

WAX PAPER

SUGAR CANE

• Green chemistry •

Materials

Corn or sugar cane biodegradable party plate
Wax-coated disposable plate
Shiny plastic disposable plate
Backyard dirt or area in a community garden (with
   permission)
Popsicle sticks
Shovel
Permanent marker

Directions

1. Dig three holes, each 12" (31cm) deep and wide
   enough to accommodate your plate size.

2. Place a plate into each hole.

3. Label each Popsicle stick with plate type (wax-
   coated, shiny or biodegradable).

4. Place Popsicle stick, like a garden stake, to mark
   location.

5. Replace dirt to bury each plate.

6. Check back in a week, a month, three months, and
   if you remember, a whole year.

Chat Point

Predict your results. How likely will it be that
the shiny disposable plate and the wax-coated
paper plate will still look the same in a year
once the dirt is brushed off? Will the disposable
shiny plate leave this earth before you do?

Mini-Chat Point

Even though you can't eat the corn or sugar
cane biodegradable party plates, they will
become dirt again. This is a perfect cycle
instead of sitting in a giant garbage pile for
hundreds of years.

Above and Beyond!

The green chemistry field of study will turn out the next generation of inventors who will make our lives more
sustainable than ever. Institutions like Yale, Carnegie Mellon and the Universities of Oregon and Vermont, to
name a notable few, have been leading the way for programs that drive innovation. High school kids will find an
environmental Mecca at www.planet-connect.org. Green issues are endless. Perhaps one future development
will be to take green chemistry in the direction of green pharmacy. Why don't we have drugs that are eco-
toxicologically benign while still maintaining their effectiveness? Onward and upward scholars!

Send Your Soles

2470010

ня **19** GANGE
TOPONTO.
131 BLOOR STREET W.
RICHARD BACH STEREO

Nike Recycling Center

c/o Reuse-A-Shoe
26755 SW 95th Ave.
Wilsonville, OR 97070

Nike Recycling Center

c/o Reuse-A-Shoe
26755 SW 95th Ave.
Wilsonville, OR 97070

Nike Recycling Cer

c/o Reuse-A-Shoe
26755 SW 95th Ave
Wilsonville, OR 970

Lochblech.schwarz

• Take that back •

Materials

Your well-worn, way-too-small sneakers, tennis shoes
 and wellies
Saved cardboard box
Marker

Directions

1. Keep a cardboard box ready to catch those athletic
   shoes that simply will not fit anymore.

2. Visit www.letmeplay.com, click on Take Action, go
   to Reuse-A-Shoe and determine whether a drop-off
   location is near you. If not, write a label and stick it on
   your collection box so it's always ready to mail when
   the box is full.

Chat Point

Support "Take Back" programs in any form
so that your used things have another life.
Nike's® Reuse-A-Shoe program is active in 10
countries. Changed habits, such as supporting a "Take Back" program are infectious!

Mini-Chat Point

Everyone has a recycling section in the
house, but if you have a "Take Back" section,
show it to your friends. Maybe they will start
one too and the whole idea will mushroom.

Above and Beyond!

There is no need to stop with shoes. Investigate **www.patagonia.com** and **www.apple.com**. Both sites have
programs incorporating the science of upcycling, whereby they take back used items that were purchased from
their store and utilize them in production processes for other items.

Materials

Paper bag, any color
Two straight sticks
Measuring tape
Unique decorations
Packing tape
Scissors
Ball of twine

Directions

1. Make a lower case "t" with the sticks.

2. Measure length and width of "t" sticks and transfer measurements to paper bag.

3. Outline perimeter of kite shape using "t" measurements as corner points.

4. Cut out kite shape.

5. Place sticks back onto the paper in the "t" form and tape in place.

6. Cut several feet of twine and string it across the shortest section of "t," knotting the string in place on one end and continuing down to bottom point.

Chat Point

Pack your homemade kite for the next waterfront expedition and combine the recycling talk with a wind-power conversation.

Mini-Chat Point

It's pretty easy to make a kite, instead of buying one — just watch out for kite-hungry trees.

7. Make kite tail with extra length of twine, adding tail decorations as desired. Include an endangered animal from an old calendar.

8. Use remaining ball of twine as handle to fly the kite.

9. Fasten the kite with numerous knots at the cross point of the twine, poking a hole with scissors through the tape to allow for the twine to be wrapped securely around the stick's cross point.

10. Wait for wind and fly!

Above and Beyond!

For insight into where kites can take us, visit **www.drachen.org** and peruse their Research section.

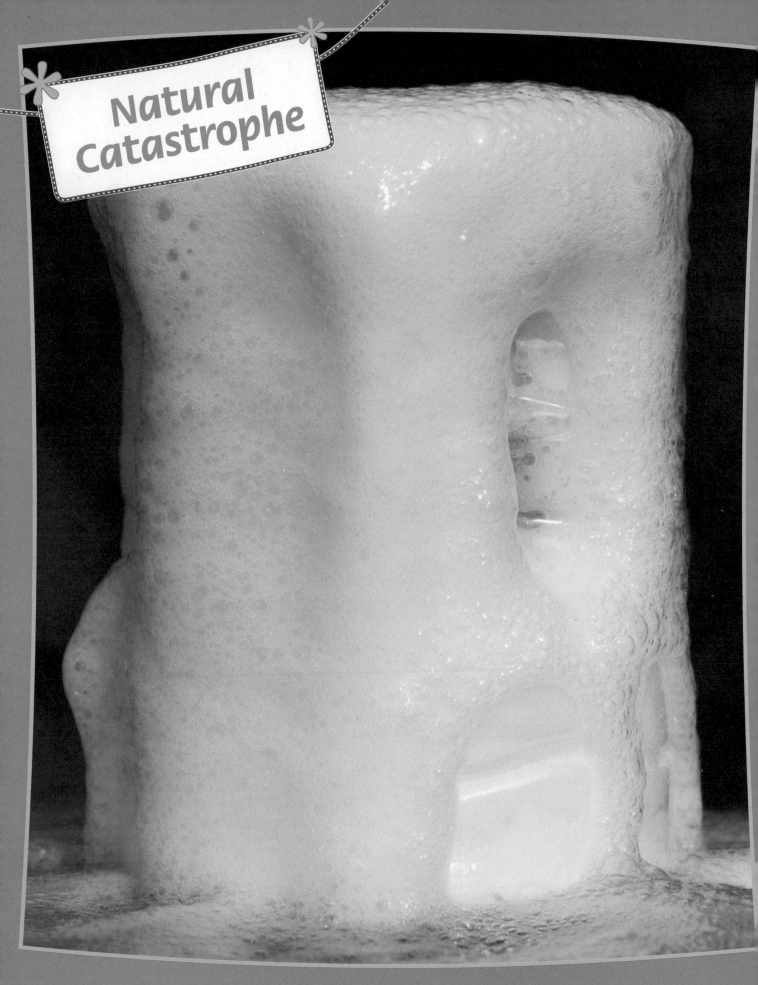

• Volcanic upheaval •

Materials

8-ounce (227g) box of baking soda
32-ounce (960ml) bottle of vinegar
Liquid dish detergent
1 large plastic recycled container
1 small plastic recycled container that will fit inside
 the large one
Tray to catch overflow

Directions

1. Set small plastic container inside larger plastic container.

2. Fill small plastic container with the entire contents of baking soda, allowing it to spill over if it exceeds the container size.

3. Add thin coating of liquid dish detergent, enough to cover the surface of the baking soda. The dishwashing liquid slows down the reaction between the vinegar and baking soda.

4. Pour vinegar directly from bottle into baking soda mixture.

5. Continue pouring until foam flows up, out and down the sides of the larger plastic container.

6. Rinse tray and repeat as often as supplies last.

Chat Point

While this imitates lava flow caused by the chemical reaction between baking soda and vinegar, real volcanoes are caused by heat and pressure deep inside the earth. Geothermal power is created by utilizing this build-up of the earth's internal heat and has the potential to eliminate the need for fossil fuels. It can provide clean, sustainable energy while protecting our environment.

Mini-Chat Point

Often a volcano will explode many, many times causing a lot of damage. Years and years later, the great lava spill becomes some of the most fertile land on earth…nature's balance.

Above and Beyond!

Take a look at **www.geo-energy.org** and discover the versatility of this inexpensive solution to powering the earth.

Solar Solutions

• Dream house •

Ingredients

10-ounce (284g) bag pretzel rods

12-ounce (340g) jar peanut butter or 8-ounce (227g) package of cream cheese ("mortar")

14.4-ounce (408g) box of graham crackers

4 fruit leather flats (**www.fruitabü.com**, sold individually or find 8 in a 3.2-ounce (91g) box)

Sharp knife

Dull butter knife

Flat dinner plate or cutting board

1" to 2" (2.5cm to 5cm) solar panel from toy kit, *optional*

Directions

1. On the flat plate or cutting board, spread a layer of mortar with the butter knife.

2. Set up house walls by setting pretzel rods like a log cabin with mortar to hold them in place. Break pretzel rods as needed to form four walls.

3. Prepare roof by spreading mortar onto one side of the graham cracker roof panels.

4. With the mortar covered side of the roof panels facing inward, carefully place into an A-frame with bottom end touching the pretzel rods and meeting at a peak. Secure with more mortar as needed.

5. Cut fruit leather flats in half.

6. With sharp knife, cut lengthwise slits into the fruit leather flats without cutting through so that it mimics a solar panel look. Add one from a toy set if possible for further effect.

7. The roof is tricky, so expect some graham crackers to break; more for the architect to eat!

8. Place prominently for viewing and eventual consumption.

Chat Point

Residential solar panels have a large upfront cost, so diligent homework is necessary to explore the options of leasing versus buying. The long-term benefits are tremendous in terms of lowering, and in some cases eliminating, electricity bills. Harnessing the sun can power a model car, charge all your electronics, light your front steps at night and more.

Mini-Chat Point

Feeling hot, hot, hot! The sun lights up our world and can light up our house too using solar panels.

Above and Beyond!

Learn more about solar technology at **www.solarcentury.com** and **www.solarcityinc.com**. Then, start your engines a new way by purchasing a super-easy solar car kit that will bring solar energy to life and make jaws drop when it really works! Visit **www.klutz.com**; search for the word "solar."

Cleans Up Nicely

• Clean slate •

Materials

Friends
Select local waterway to make litter-free
Extra-large garden bags for disposing of litter
Pointy sticks for stabbing garbage
Straight sticks for chopstick-like action to pick up
   other litter types

Directions

1. Organize date and place to meet with garden bags
   in hand.

2. Seek appropriate sticks in the vicinity.

3. Work as long as possible and dispose of filled
   garden bags appropriately.

4. Admire results.

Chat Point

A little sweat equity among friends goes a long way in protecting the value of natural resources.

Mini-Chat Point

Hopefully, you'll never see someone toss garbage out of their car. It would begin a journey from the street where it landed all the way into the water supply with a little help from some rain clouds. That's not where you want to see it.

Above and Beyond!

For a vivid display of the garbage finds along our highways, waterways and even on our yards, set aside a package tray leftover from organic fruits or vegetables and keep the plastic store-wrap with the bar code and sticker on it. Place some of your garbage finds such as bottle caps, cigarette butts, candy wrappers and plastic pieces onto the food tray. Wrap the reserved findings with the reserved plastic store-wrap and display. By making and displaying several packages of litter, it has a naturally offensive and unappealing impact. Somehow, packaged as a food item, the human response seems to be a resounding "that's not right!" Visit www.surfrider.org to discover their strategic initiatives when it comes to water and beach areas.

Not a Day Too Soon, 2000s

Dear Restaurant Owner,

Our whole family enjoys eating at your restaurant whenever we are in your town. We celebrate many occasions around your extra large family-size tables, covered in beautiful linens, appointed with cloth napkins folded just right and sparkling silverware. Your extra tasty red pepper dipping oil for brick oven bread is always eagerly anticipated and so much consumed that we always wonder who will actually eat dinner. But it always happens, with pleasant conversations, people we know stopping by to say hello, sitting amidst all the black and white photos of your own family heritage. Somehow there is still room for dessert, at least until we are faced with the enormous slice of cheesecake or giant bowl of cannoli gelato with extra wafers. It all makes for a warm and wonderful family dining experience.

Then one day, as we were traveling through, without having the time for a leisurely family sit-down dinner, we decided we should try your take-out since we knew the food would be exceptional....and it was. However, the foamed polystyrene containers were a sad surprise. While we know that no restauranteur wants their expertly prepared meal sticking to the container, there are alternatives that will not live in the landfill forever and ever. Foamed polystyrene is not recyclable and in many cities in the western United States, it is banned altogether. While alternatives such as corn and sugar cane based take-out containers are expensive, they are biodegradable. Our idea for you is to start offering them when phone orders come in for a small charge while you go through a phase out period. After that, you can charge a take-out surcharge explaining it as similar to a 'fuel surcharge' that so many services were charging when gas prices went up. Your food has such a loyal following that a take-out surcharge is not going to make or break the decision to eat there. Citizens concerned about the state of our foamed polystyrene world will happily pay it and others will be learning and becoming aware of alternatives that simply make sense since one day there will not be an alternative. Thank you for considering new takeout containers!

Materials

A computer at home, school, office or library
Permission to change the margin format permanently

Directions

1. Follow Page Setup or similar icon on your computer to change the side margins of every page from 1.25" (3.8cm) to 0.50" (1.25cm).

Chat Point

Slow down paper waste, save money and preserve an acre. Use the back of school notices and other single-sided papers to print drafts, only when necessary, to stretch your conservation even further.

Mini-Chat Point

Who decided to leave so much of the paper blank when a computer prints it?

 Above and Beyond!

Check out **www.changethemargins.com** and under Campaign Info click on Sign the Microsoft® Petition to save some trees and/or write a letter to your boss, principal, aunt — anyone who prints. For more paper-saving information, go to **www.papercalculator.org**.

Home Invasion

• Unsolicited takeover •

Materials

Computer printout of a photograph of your house or apartment
Existing houseplant in a pot
2 branches, twigs or Popsicle sticks, approx. 6" long
Hot glue gun
Cutting of a local invasive plant species

Directions

1. Plug in glue gun to preheat.

2. Place paper photograph facedown.

3. Glue sticks, spaced apart, on bottom of paper. (Be sure the house is facing upward so sticks are glued to the bottom of the house photograph.)

4. Poke bottom end of sticks into the dirt of houseplant.

5. Swirl and wind the local invasive plant cutting around the house photo.

Above and Beyond!

To learn about a range of invasive species issues and what's happening in your neighborhood in the U.S. and internationally, visit www.invasivespeciesinfo.gov.

Materials

Leaves from local trees
Glue stick
Cardboard
Paper
Markers, crayons or computer available for printing labels
Library book about tree leaf identification

Directions

1. Spread out the local leaf collection on the cardboard.

2. Using the leaf identification book, determine the correct name for each leaf.

3. If you run into difficulties, seek out a gardener or visit a botanical garden with your leaf samples.

4. Glue leaves directly onto the cardboard.

5. Create labels for the leaves with marker or print out speak bubbles with tree names.

6. Glue labels on or next to appropriate leaves.

Chat Point

Give your local trees an identity and it will become second nature to care for them when they seem diseased or if someone wants to remove them without good reason.

Mini-Chat Point

The more you get to know your family of trees, the better. Notice when the maple turns a brighter red than last year and if the oak tree loses its leaves much earlier than it did before. What is growing on the bark of the gingko? Why did that one branch on the white pine die over the winter?

Above and Beyond!

Seek and find local programs like Adopt-A-Tree to contribute to the continuation of tree families. To see how New York City is spreading its branches, check out **www.milliontreesnyc.org**.

• Don't water it down •

Materials

Pennies of any denomination
Water dropper
Water
Small bowl
Flat, even surface

Directions

1. Line up the pennies on a flat, even surface.

2. Fill small bowl with water.

3. Prepare water dropper with water.

4. Slowly count the number of drops that will fit onto the face of the penny before overflowing.

Chat Point

Think about President Abraham Lincoln as you see his face on the penny filled with water. How much different do you think his quality of water was when he lived compared to what we have now. What has happened since he lived is astounding. Today, chemicals numbering in the thousands have been added to our daily life each year, and their ultimate place of rest is in our waterways.

Mini-Chat Point

If you could ask President Abraham Lincoln anything about his life when he was little, what would you ask?

Above and Beyond!

Learn about Do-It-Yourself water testing with kits available from your local hardware store. Look up the meaning of the elements analyzed. Run the same test on water fountains at school, your place of work, the fitness club, etc. When traveling, consult www.safewateronline.com.

Pollution Resolution

Materials

Small, glass containers to place on the outer windowsill of each window of your house or apartment

Small-size jars from lip balm or make-up products (heat resistant containers)

16-ounce (454g) jar coconut oil (www.spectrumorganics.com)

Small saucepan

Spoon

Directions

1. Coconut oil is solid at around 73°F (23°C). It will have to be liquefied to fit into the small containers at an even height.

2. Using the spoon, dig out an estimated quantity that will fill your small containers when melted.

3. Place the solid coconut oil into saucepan.

4. Warm up over low heat until liquefied.

5. Set small containers in a row and carefully add liquid coconut oil to fill each one.

6. Allow to set for an hour or less.

7. Once solid and white in color, place one container on the outside sill of each one of your windows.

8. Leave the containers outside for a weekday and weekend day (Friday-Saturday or Sunday-Monday) so all traffic patterns are covered.

9. When you bring the containers back into the house, note which window containers have more air pollution markings on them and which window containers show a pure white solid.

10. Based on your evidence, figure out which windows you should open to air out the house, with cross-breeze strategy in mind, leaving the most polluted windows out of the equation.

Chat Point

Air quality can be deceiving if you are not situated near a factory spewing the obvious black smoke. Newspapers and Web sites track air quality, from allergens to smog, and viewing their assessments is a good idea before exercising in poor air quality conditions. Just as you often cannot see the poor air quality mentioned in news outlets, you may be missing the pollution right outside your window. You may find that your front-facing windows invite the most exhaust pollution from cars going by, or your rear-facing windows may be in a wind stream directly from a factory that you don't see. Not all carcinogens are black, brown or visible, but you'll likely discover something by conducting your own experiment. Opening the windows where the least pollution enters the house would be the best choice for airing out the house when the weather is beautiful.

Mini-Chat Point

This experiment also can be done with any leftover petroleum jelly you have in the house. Hopefully, it will be your last jar, as eliminating any product with dinosaur wine (oil and its products) is a huge step in the right direction for sustainable living.

Above and Beyond!

Check local weather Web sites for detailed allergy and pollution information. Specifics can be found at **www.airnow.gov**, including vacation destinations you may want to analyze if you're planning a trip.

• *Makes my hair stand on end* •

Materials

8 cups (2kg) or more of potting soil or compost

2 cups (454g) grass seed

1 pair worn-out socks

1 large, clear plastic water bottle, rescued out of recycling

Small garden trowel

Running water

Marker

Watering can

If indoors: bathtub

If outdoors: small ground area with dirt

Directions

1. Cut off the top spout of plastic water bottle, making an even opening.

2. Using trowel, fill with soil or compost, almost to the brim. Set aside.

3. Put socks on your feet.

4. Place stocking feet under running water.

5. Spread grass seed in bathtub or on dirt.

6. Walk over the grass seed until most seeds are adhered to the socks.

7. Carefully remove socks, trying to keep grass seeds in place.

8. Place the socks, grass-seed side up, on top of the soil or compost in the plastic bottle.

9. Using trowel, scrape small amounts of soil or compost onto the sock to aid in germination.

10. Water slowly and carefully with a watering can.

11. Draw a face on the outside of the plastic water bottle.

12. Place on windowsill that gets as much sun exposure as possible.

13. Water every few days and watch for fresh, green blades of grass.

Chat Point

The green, grass lawns of suburbia require excessive amounts of watering. Reducing (or eliminating — gasp!) your lawn size and using native plantings will still result in fine garden design and allow for natural drought and flood adaptability.

Mini-Chat Point

Goats and sheep keep grass trimmed very nicely and they fertilize it at the same time. Since they aren't likely to become your landscapers, ask about gas-free push mowers.

Above and Beyond!

Retire your gas-powered lawn mower and check out www.neutonpower.com. Battery-operated mowers work beautifully after a full charge. They are very quiet and you won't offend any neighbors when you cut the lawn at 6:00 a.m.

Walking a Tightrope

• *Trickle down effect* •

Materials

Pitcher, measuring cup or dish with a handle and
  spout
1 foot (31cm) of twine
Packing tape
Cup
Tray to catch overflow

Directions

1. Tape one end of twine securely to the handle of a
   pitcher, measuring cup or dish.

2. Fill with water.

3. Place free end of string over spout end, extending
   down into cup.

4. Lifting pitcher up, have one participant pull twine
   taut, resting carefully within the cup.

5. Carefully start to pour the water one trickle at a
   time, finding the right angle, to send drops down
   the twine and fill the cup.

Chat Point

Our planet's water supply is walking a tightrope and performing quite a balancing act in the process. The show does not go on forever and there are no hidden safety mats to catch the problems. Groundwater contamination, acid rain and commercial dumping are a few of the serious threats to our clean water supplies.

Mini-Chat Point

Tell your teachers about World Water Monitoring Day™. See Web site information below.

Above and Beyond!

Do your part to help with the World Water Monitoring program at **www.worldwatermonitoringday.org**.

• Family tree •

Materials

Time to take a walk in your neighborhood or park in search of a tree stump.

Directions

1. Once you find a tree stump where a tree recently has been felled, stop and count the rings.

2. Count back the years to when you were born. Is the tree as old or older than you?

Chat Point

The easiest thing you can do is plant a tree to call your own as you grow up. If you do not have a garden, using a pot for a seedling works just as well and they make great gifts. Find what grows well in your area as a native plant and put the shovel in the ground.

Mini-Chat Point

Find a favorite tree. Think about who might have hugged that tree before you did? What were they wearing and how old do you think they were? Did anyone climb it or swing in it? There is a whole life story in each tree.

Above and Beyond!

Local groups make a big difference in tree planting efforts as does **www.treesponsibility.com** in Calderdale, England. You can help from anywhere in the world by supporting efforts to plant a billion trees in the Atlantic Forest of Brazil, **www.plantabillion.org**.

Like Oil and Water

KISS my FACE

organic

Treated

• Bad hair day •

Materials

½ cup (120ml) olive or vegetable oil
Comb
Sink
Old kitchen towel
Mirror
Shower

Directions

1. Using a comb, part your hair in the middle and leave one side as is.

2. On the other half, bend over a sink and pour oil onto your hair to coat.

3. Place an old kitchen towel over the shoulder located under the oily half of hair.

4. Look in the mirror.

5. Reflect on Chat Point.

6. Wash out in shower with recommended shampoo noted in Above and Beyond!

Chat Point

Imagine how difficult it must have been for all creatures engulfed in oil when human error caused oil spills of gargantuan proportions affecting their habitats.

Mini-Chat Point

Oily hair may not look nice, but having to swim in oil sounds much worse. Many people volunteer to help creatures that suffer when humans cause disasters like oil spills in our waterways.

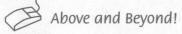 **Above and Beyond!**

For organic hair care that is up for the task of removing more than the average amount of oil from hair, go to **www.kissmyface.com**. Look under Products/Organic Hair Care and scroll down to Miss Treated® Shampoo to find understandable, organic ingredients to tackle your sticky situation. Lather, rinse and repeat under the low-flow shower head.

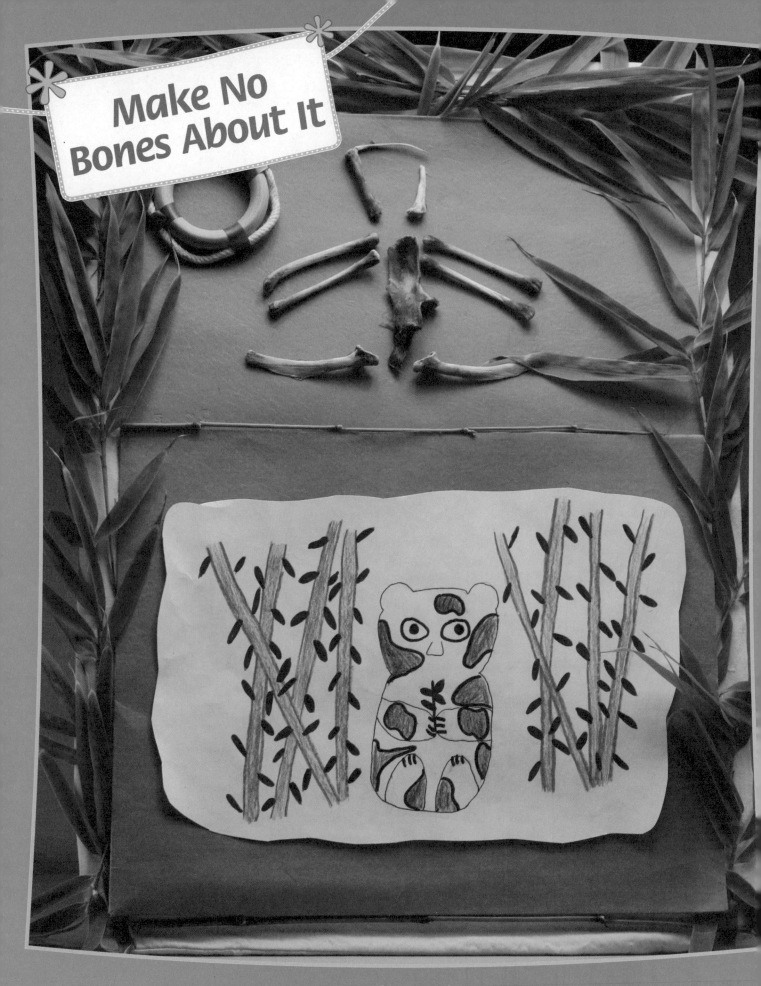

Make No Bones About It

• Save the panda •

Materials

1 roasted chicken carcass
Dish towel
Cardboard box, cut to manageable size
Hot glue gun
Markers or crayons

Directions

1. After enjoying a roasted chicken, pick the bones as clean as possible.

2. Wash and dry the bones until they are meat free.

3. Set aside the carcass to air-dry while you prepare the cardboard.

4. Plug in hot glue gun.

5. Conduct an Internet search to find an endangered species animal that you would like to see on this earth for many more years. Try searching www.worldwildlife.org.

6. Using markers, draw the outline of the animal onto the cardboard.

7. With a pencil, sketch in the skeleton bones. It does not have to be scientifically accurate, just enough to show the animal outline.

8. Write a creative title such as "No More Dinosaurs" or "Save the Snow Leopard."

9. Include a fact about why this animal is considered endangered.

10. Arrange the chicken bones in a way to cover the skeleton lines and erase any extra lines.

11. Using the hot glue gun, firmly attach the bones to the cardboard and allow to dry in place.

Chat Point

Learn about habitat destruction to find out where you can help in saving your endangered animal of choice. The animal's only advocates are people like you who first take the time to learn about them and then contribute to the action of saving them. Write to your local newspaper. Find a public radio station willing to devote a short time to your topic. Join a local conservation group or nature center to keep habitats healthy for your local species too, some of which may be threatened as well.

Mini-Chat Point

Bones are so fascinating and they show part of what holds an animal together on the inside. Dinosaur bones are still being discovered today. We never even had the chance to meet the dinosaurs. We don't want delightful creatures like the snow leopard, swordfish and hippopotamus to become like dinosaurs and only be featured in movies instead of alive and well.

Above and Beyond!

Visit www.paleoportal.org and check out the fossil gallery of animals that used to be here. At www.bagheera.com, under the News section, you'll find the latest information about turtle babies, whale sightings, the status of the gray wolves and much more.

Save the Polar Bears

• On thin ice •

Steps 1 and 2 require a sleepover in the freezer

Materials

Any small plastic or stuffed Arctic animals found
 around the house
2 to 3 glass baking pans
Ice cube trays filled with water and frozen
Red-cabbage-colored water (See Getting Started
 section, page 7.)

Directions

1. Make colored water following directions on page 7.
   (Water will be blue.)

2. Pour colored water into each glass baking pan to a
   depth of 1" to 1½" (3cm to 4cm).

3. Place in freezer overnight.

4. Remove blue ocean water pans from the freezer
   and set in a central display location.

5. Empty out ice cube trays and arrange as icebergs
   on top of blue ice.

6. Place Arctic animals on ice floes and periodically
   observe throughout the day.

Chat Point

What do you think will happen to the
animals? If all the ice melts, where will they
go? Will they have far to swim? Will it be too
far to swim if they don't have any resting
spots on other ice floes? If they're too tired,
will they be able to pursue their dinner?

Mini-Chat Point

It sounds like the polar bear is in trouble.
The polar bear can't email the decision-
makers to put an end to things that make
global warming happen, so it's up to us.

Above and Beyond!

Search for "eight ways to green your road trip" at **www.edf.org** as another way to reduce consumption on your
next trip. For traveling locally, try to walk, bike, rollerblade, scooter or skateboard whenever possible and safe to
do so.

SunDrops Global Warming Bingo

Materials

Bag of plain chocolate or peanut SunDrops
 (or similar product)
4 sheets of recycled paper large enough to make
 5" x 5" (13cm x 13cm) squares
4 sheets of 8½" x 11" (22cm x 28cm) recycled paper
Ruler
Glue
Scissors
Pen or computer
Serving bowl

Directions

1. Using ruler, scissors and recycled paper, cut four 5" x 5" (13cm x 13cm) squares to make four bingo playing cards.

2. Glue the 5" x 5" (13cm x 13cm) squares onto the 8½" x 11" (22cm x 28cm) sheets of paper.

3. Using a ruler, mark off 1" (2.5cm) segments, across and down each card to create a grid of 25 boxes.

4. Pen in words or phrases relating to global warming in the boxes using some words or phrases pictured and others of choice, ensuring that each card has a different order of words or phrases in the boxes.

5. Pour SunDrops (or similar product) into serving bowl and place in the middle of the gaming table.

6. Players use SunDrops (or similar product) to mark their cards when a parent or a friend calls out the global warming word or phrase.

7. Bingo!

Chat Point

With movies, speeches, emails, press coverage and video footage, the word is getting out. Sailing ice-free through the Northwest Passage was unthinkable for decades, but here we are in present times with trade and tourist boats passing through unhindered by the elements. To help suppress the rapid ice melting, change a habit today. Plant a tree, write to government officials to curb greenhouse gas emissions and make a difference.

Mini-Chat Point

Global warming seems like such a big problem for grown-ups. And yes, they do need to take care of the big things like making new rules about energy and cars, but little people count too, because it will be your planet for a long time. Share the habits you learn in this book with your family, friends and teachers.

Above and Beyond!

Visit the influential campaign at **www.stopglobalwarming.org** and check out the video section choices. Until global warming affects people's daily lives, it's easy to keep it at arm's length. Professional skiers and snowboarders see the effects first, as winter has been compromised in the Andes, the Rockies, the Himalayas and the Alps.

Take a Dive

• *Reverse our planet's nose dive* •

Materials

Flippers
Friends or family
Planet Earth 5-disc movie set (rent it)
Goggles or scuba wear

Directions

1. Wear flippers and goggles.

2. Watch Planet Earth's water and coral footage.

3. Have a race with flippers on.

Chat Point

The race is on to save the coral reefs that are dying off around the world. As a result of warming ocean temperatures, algae grows more profusely and stunts the coral lives. Though it may seem disconnected, any sustainable habit you change like buying organic (no matter how you spell it) helps the coral reef. Revolutions are started by one.

Mini-Chat Point

Help save the beautiful coral and the fish that call it home. Everything you do to help the earth makes a difference.

Above and Beyond!

For answers to most diving questions, visit www.montereybayaquarium.org and search for "discover diving."

Go Plastic-Free for a Day

• Wanted: Alternatives! •

Materials to do Without

ATM or credit card purchases (eek!)
Computer (ugh!)
Plastic or nalgene bottles (thirsty!)
Plastic toys, kids and dogs (what now?)
Toothbrush (yikes!)

Directions

1. Spend a whole day plastic free.

2. Make a list of the hurdles plastic presents.

3. Analyze what can come off the list completely or have a sustainable alternative.

Chat Point

One little-old day without plastic sounds easy enough until you start bumping into plastic everywhere like the wrapper on the morning newspaper, the yogurt container at breakfast, the laundry detergent bottle and the cheese wrapper staring at you in the grocery store. Eliminating even one plastic component in your daily life is a step in the right direction. Don't buy new plastic if at all possible, and use existing containers to store items.

Mini-Chat Point

For a change of pace, play with toys from **www.vermontwoodentoys.com**.

Above and Beyond!

If you have a retail or online business, check into the credit card processing services of **www.dharmamerchantservices.com**.

• Low grass mileage •

Materials

Email account

Driveway, garage, backyard, or approved park or
 schoolyard space

Numerous, separated plants from your own garden
 (have extras for exchange or to give away)

Extra pots or paper bags for transporting plants

Soil

Compost

Trowels

A few old towels for dirty hands

Fresh-squeezed lemonade, pitcher and tumblers

Directions

1. Organize a plant exchange.

2. Email your invitation with details of when, where
   and what to bring. Try to include a garden-club
   member or other expert to be on hand to answer
   questions.

3. What to bring list should include trowel, two to
   three favorite plants separated from their host
   plant (place in smaller pot or brown paper bags for
   moving) ready to exchange for new plants.

4. Ask guests to label the plant and provide general
   instructions for light and water before arriving.

5. Make fresh-squeezed lemonade and have available
   in pitcher, with tumblers.

6. On day of exchange set out your own plants on a
   table or on the ground to get things started.

7. Arrange trowels, pots, towels, soil and compost
   separately in user-friendly fashion.

Chat Point

While you hear a lot about food miles, plant miles count too when considering fossil fuels that are being used to transport plants from far and wide to garden nurseries and grocery stores. Organizing a community, family or school plant exchange brings new life to everyone's home or garden. Set aside a section of plants to donate to a local charity, such as Habitat for Humanity®, soliciting volunteers before they depart to help plant around the new or renovated homes.

Mini-Chat Point

A party with dirt, shovels and lemonade beats a trip to the garden nursery where hours can be lost while adults look around and make up their minds about which plants to buy. You saved a plant the trip on a train, plane or truck!

Above and Beyond!

In addition to cutting down on tremendous plant mileage, any new plants that you bring indoors will have a positive effect on indoor air quality. Plants such as aloe vera, ficus and spider plants are just some that work to cleanse the air. Visit **www.lungusa.org** and search for "indoor air quality" to learn what may be lurking in your airspace.

THE LAB REPORT
COMPLETION CHART
(science projects)

Give Yourself a Hand

Give yourself a hand for understanding more about how to be a good citizen and help save the planet. Every small step you take in reducing your carbon footprint as you walk through Mother Earth's learning activities is a step to a better world. Color or note each branch as you complete the project. Branches are numbered.

Section 2: The Kitchen Sink
(food projects)

Experience sustainable taste sensations together in the kitchen. Make a dinner-version birthday cake, frosted with organic mashed potatoes and topped with beeswax candles to celebrate the planet we all call home. Find yourselves laughing back at the whale face made out of a watermelon. Lick your fingers after painting rose leaves with fair trade chocolate. Put on an apron, or get messy and find the tie-ins to green living habits in every bite.

Chili Ristra

• Piping hot •

Ristra Materials

12 to 15 chili peppers of all colors and varieties
12" (31cm) twine for hanging
12 to 15 strips of twine 4" (10cm) long for knotting
  peppers in place
Scissors

Directions

1. Using the 12" (31cm) piece of twine, make a loop
   for hanging and knot in place at one end.

2. With the small strips of twine, knot pepper stems in
   place down the 12" (31cm) length of twine.

3. Hang in the kitchen.

4. Snip and use for chili, or for decorative purposes.

Shriveling will occur naturally and it adds character.

Chili Hot Chocolate Ingredients

Serves 1
8 ounces (240ml) milk
1 teaspoon (2g) Green & Black's® Cocoa Powder
  (or similar brand)
¼ bar of a 3.5-ounce (18g) Green & Black's Maya
  Gold™ chocolate bar, chopped (or similar brand)
2 tablespoons (25g) sugar
¼ teaspoon (0.6g) cinnamon
Pinch of ground chili pepper

Directions

1. Warm milk in a saucepan until steam begins to
   form (do not allow to boil over).

2. Add chopped chocolate and sugar and stir.

3. Stir in cinnamon and ground chili pepper.

COCOA POWDER

GREEN &BLACK'S

ORGANIC

MADE FROM
ORGANIC
BEANS

USDA
ORGANIC

Chat Point

Mexican markets have many varieties of chili peppers ranging in flavor from mild to fiery hot. Chili peppers are consumed in great numbers and are another example of a crop that needs bees for essential cross-pollination. Running out of chili peppers is not an option and would pose a natural culinary catastrophe in some countries.

Mini-Chat Point

Nature is an amazing spice rack. Using organic spices eliminates a pinch of pesticide ending up on your favorite food.

Above and Beyond!

Check your findings on fumigation and irradiation of spices at **www.forestrade.com**, a supplier of organic and sustainably produced tropical spices, vanilla, essential oils, and Fair Trade coffee, based in Vermont.

Chocolate Orange Pudding

• Orange you glad I didn't say banana? •

Ingredients

Serves 8

6 oranges (2 are extras, mistakes with holes and tilting
  can eliminate some from being available to hold the
  chocolate pudding)
1 package, 5 ounces (128g) organic chocolate
  pudding (www.oetker.us)
2 tablespoons (12g) orange zest
Grater
Baking dish
Knife
Cutting board
Spoon

Directions

1. Cut oranges in half and juice them, refrigerating the juice for other uses.

2. Scoop out remaining pulp from the orange halves, carefully avoiding making a hole in the bottom of each orange half.

3. Level off the bottom of any orange half that tilts too much, again without making a hole in the bottom.

4. Prepare pudding according to package directions.

5. Grate zest from two of the extra orange halves and add to warm pudding.

6. Place orange halves into a baking dish that will fit into the refrigerator.

7. Pour pudding into each orange, filling to the brim.

8. Refrigerate until set.

Chat Point

Use the whole orange by tossing the empty halves, post-chocolate pudding consumption, into the fire pit or fireplace for a fresh orange scent. Cutting circles out of the orange halves, stringing them with ribbon and hanging to dry makes a naturally scented decoration.

Mini-Chat Point

Knock, knock, "Who's there?" Banana.
Knock, knock, "Who's there?" Banana.
Knock, knock, "Who's there?" Banana.
Knock, knock, "Who's there?"
Orange you glad I didn't say banana!

Above and Beyond!

Visit **www.organicvalley.com**, click on Organic Juice and find three types of orange juice as well as numerous choices of organic milk and other wholesome products.

Like a Great Pizza Pie

Ingredients

Serves 8
Refrigerated pizza dough (**www.Trader Joe's®.com**)
16 ounces (227g) cream cheese
18-ounce (510g) jar strawberry or raspberry jam
Assorted fruits
Butter knife

Directions

1. Bake pizza crust according to directions and set aside to cool.

2. Slice fruit selections into attractive shapes.

3. Using the butter knife, spread cream cheese over the pizza leaving the edges clear.

4. Spread the jam around the edges to resemble a real pizza pie.

5. Dot with fruit for a new kind of pizza pie.

Chat Point

Take a slice out of your exposure to polytetrafluoroethylene (brand name Teflon®). Avoid pizza out of a Teflon-coated pizza box. If the box is shiny, it likely is Teflon-coated so your pizza slips right off. Teflon can be found in the blood of most Americans and is reason enough to eat your pizza in the restaurant instead of taking it out, when you have the choice.

Mini-Chat Point

Nonstick can make you sick!

Above and Beyond!

Check **www.foodnews.org** for a listing of pesticide-doused fruits, and choose organic counterparts instead.

Apple Cranberry Pie

• Pie swap •

Ingredients

Serves 8

16-ounce (454g) box of frozen phyllo (twin pack of
  9" x 14" (23cm x 36cm) sheets)
1 cup (95g) whole cranberries
2 cans of 21-ounce (12.5kg) apple pie filling or 2 cups
  (250g) peeled, chopped apples
½ cup (110g) brown sugar
¼ cup (31g) flour
½ teaspoon (1.5g) cinnamon
¾ cup (34g) bread crumbs
½ cup (120ml) butter, melted
Damp towel
Pastry brush
Springform pan
Nonstick spray
Powdered sugar

Directions

1. Preheat oven to 400°F (204°C).

2. If frozen, defrost phyllo dough to room temperature.

3. Carefully, unroll phyllo dough and keep a damp towel over unused portion after each piece is removed.

4. Mix together cranberries, apple pie filling and cinnamon.

5. Spray springform pan with nonstick spray.

6. Place two or three layers of phyllo dough on bottom of springform pan to cover and line edges.

7. Dip pastry brush in melted butter and spread over phyllo dough.

8. Sprinkle all the bread crumbs over this first layer.

9. Add another layer of phyllo dough sheets and spread melted butter.

10. Place ½ cup (48g) of cranberries on this layer and another layer of phyllo, follow with butter.

11. Spoon one 21-ounce (12.5kg) can of apple pie filling over the next layer, followed by phyllo and butter.

12. Continue layering until all ingredients have been added, always separating with a layer of phyllo dough and butter.

13. End with multiple layers of phyllo dough and butter, folding up and over ingredients.

14. Bake for 15 minutes at 400°F (204°C).

15. Reduce temperature to 350°F (177°C), loosely cover with foil and bake for an additional 45 minutes.

16. Let cool.

17. Carefully remove from pan to serving plate.

18. Sprinkle with powdered sugar.

Chat Point

What better way to encourage home baking with locally grown fruits than to have a pie swap? Kids' versions can use any number of the frozen wheat or white organic pie crusts available and their favorite fillings.

Mini-Chat Point

Using locally grown fruits to make a pie is a great way to support your nearby farmer. Baking what is in season makes good sense too, so watch the harvest choices change throughout the year along with the pie flavors.

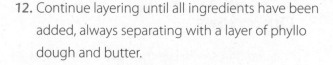 ### Above and Beyond

Send an invitation with complete details and a scanned photo of your pie via email to your guests. Better still, use **www.evite.com** which will encourage the recipients to consider the service for themselves instead of using written invitations for the next get-together.

Egg Carton Pizza Garden

• *Grow your own toppings* •

Materials

1 empty egg carton
Herb seeds or young plantings
Soil or compost to fill egg carton
Trowel

Later Date After Successful Herb Growth

Plain cheese pizza of choice
Pizza cutter
Clean, small scissors

Directions

1. If planting seeds, use the trowel to set up the egg carton with soil or compost.

2. Add seeds, pressing into soil or compost.

3. If using young plantings, arrange in egg carton compartments, adding soil or compost as needed.

4. Place on a windowsill, watering every other day to dampen, not soak.

5. After a few inches of growth, plan a pizza party.

6. Prepare herbs by setting egg carton in the middle of the table, accompanied by clean, small scissors.

7. Order or make favorite plain cheese pizzas for guests.

8. Serve hot pizzas and encourage guests to "snip and serve" fresh herb additions to top off their personalized pizza portions.

Chat Point

Rosemary, basil and oregano are typical accompaniments to the ingredients found in pizza. Be bold and try cilantro, chives or even edible flowers. It will not be just another pizza party night. Extra herbs? Freeze with water in an ice cube tray for future flavorful cooking.

Mini-Chat Point

Trying herbs a little at a time will open the door to a world of exciting flavors. See if you're ready to have a small herb garden in an outdoor container or in your yard.

Above and Beyond!

Herbs are renowned for their multi-tasking abilities. Their contribution to healthy teas comes in the form of offering medicinal benefits and plain comfort on a cold day. Milder herbs and child-sized proportions are used in the Just For Kids line from tea masters, **www.traditionalmedicinals.com**. Their full range of adult sipping choices is outstanding.

Lemon Freeze

• Organic sun-kissed •

Ingredients

Serves 12

8 lemons (There are 2 extra, as mistakes with holes
   and tilting can eliminate some from being available
   to hold the lemon freeze)

3 cups (720ml) heavy cream

½ cup (120ml) lemon juice from squeezed lemons

1¼ cups (284g) sugar

3 tablespoons (18g) lemon zest

Large mixing bowl

Grater

Baking dish

Knife

Cutting board

Spoon

Directions

1. Cut all eight lemons in half and juice them.

2. Scoop out remaining pulp from the lemon halves,
   carefully avoiding making a hole in the bottom of
   each lemon half.

3. Level off the bottom of any lemon half that tilts too
   much to hold liquid, again without making a hole
   in the bottom.

4. Using two of the extra halves that may be
   imperfect or suffered a hole, grate lemon zest into a
   large mixing bowl.

5. Add heavy cream, lemon juice and sugar. Refrigerate
   remaining lemon juice for other uses.

6. Set lemon halves into a baking dish that will fit into
   the freezer.

7. Pour heavy cream mixture into each lemon, filling
   to the brim.

8. Freeze overnight and up to one month.

9. Serve frozen.

Chat Point

If the lemon freeze is served with just a
spoon, the whole fruit serves a purpose and
some dish water and soap is saved along the
way. Make a list of other all-in-one fruits that
could be used for serving dessert, vegetables
and appetizers.

Mini-Chat Point

When life gives you conventional lemons,
pass over them and make organic lemonade.

Above and Beyond!

Lemon is also a natural cleaner so instead of reaching under the sink to clean and treat your wood floors and furniture,
reach into the fruit bowl and test a simple homemade formula of ½ cup (120ml) olive oil mixed with ½ cup (120ml)
lemon juice. Search for "lemons" at **www.healthychild.org** and learn many more uses for lemons.

Prantipos

• Not just peanuts •

Ingredients

Yields approx. 36 cookies

1 cup (258g) smooth or chunky organic peanut butter
½ cup (118ml) maple syrup
½ cup (170g) liquid honey
½ cup (128g) smooth applesauce
2 small mashed bananas
3 tablespoons (45ml) vegetable oil
1½ teaspoons (7.5ml) vanilla extract
1½ cups (186g) white flour
¾ cup (90g) whole-wheat flour
1 teaspoon (5g) baking powder
1 teaspoon (5g) baking soda
¾ cup (126g) semisweet chocolate chips
½ cup (55g) dried cranberries
Nonstick spray
Cookie sheet

Directions

1. Preheat oven to 350°F (177°C).

2. Spray cookie sheet with nonstick spray.

3. Mix all ingredients until blended.

4. Place on cookie sheet in heaping teaspoonfuls.

5. Bake for 11 minutes.

Chat Point

A lot of power is packed into this cookie. Organic peanut butter is a highlight, as organic peanuts have avoided contributing to pesticide-contaminated groundwater from methyl bromide used in the growing process of conventional peanuts.

Mini-Chat Point

What a funny name for a cookie. It's short for the protein found in the peanut butter, the antioxidants (disease fighting parts) found in dried cranberries and the potassium in the bananas. Big cheer!

Above and Beyond!

Check out **www.drgreene.com** and search for "organic Rx peanut butter." You will discover what is crowding out the peanuts on the conventional peanut butter labels and the health benefits of this cool nut…that is actually a legume.

Speltapple Muffins

365 ORGANIC™
EVERYDAY VALUE

Organic
Unbleached
White Spelt
Flour

WHOLE FOODS
MARKET

USDA ORGANIC

NET WT 2 LBS (907g)

• Is that spelt right? •

Ingredients

Yields 12 muffins

½ cup (120ml) vegetable oil

1 cup (145g) brown sugar

2 eggs

2 tablespoons (30ml) milk

2 cups (220g) chopped, peeled apple chunks

1½ cups (180g) spelt flour

1 teaspoon (5g) baking soda

1 teaspoon (5g) baking powder

½ teaspoon (1.2g) cinnamon

Muffin tin sprayed with nonstick spray

Topping

1 teaspoon (2.3g) cinnamon

1½ tablespoons (19g) white sugar

Directions

1. Preheat oven to 375°F (190°C).

2. In a large bowl, beat oil, sugar, eggs and milk.

3. Stir in apples to coat.

4. Sift dry ingredients together in measuring cup.

5. Add dry ingredients to mixture.

6. Stir well and fill greased muffin tin.

7. Mix cinnamon and sugar for topping.

8. Sprinkle topping on batter and bake for 20 minutes.

Chat Point

Spelt is a grain that has been around forever. It is by its very nature more resistant to pests and disease than wheat. It also grows with less fertilizer so its entire composition is easier on the earth. Substitute for all-purpose or whole-wheat flour. Although it may not raise sky high, the taste is lofty and not at all compromising.

Mini-Chat Point

Spelt grows in a field like wheat or corn. It is ground into flour and can be used in many recipes. It is very high in protein that your body needs for good health. Look for it in the store and see if it is spelled right.

Above and Beyond!

Spend some time at www.wholefoodsmarket.com and search for spelt flour recipes.

Materials

Sweet-toothed friends
Agave nectar
Maple syrup
2 small cups
Chopsticks or small spoons for each sweetener
  multiplied by the number of friends sampling
Small plate
Blindfold bandana
Pencil
Paper

Directions

1. Without your sweet-toothed friends in sight, set out cups and add a different sweetener to each one, remembering which one is in the cup or noting it on the bottom of the cups.

2. Have a set of chopsticks ready for each participant.

3. Place the small plate within reach so that all used chopsticks can go in one place.

4. Blindfold one participant at a time and instruct to taste test both sweeteners and give descriptive opinions, as in wine tasting.

5. Determine a taste-test winner between the two sweeteners.

Chat Point

The world of nature provides so many interesting textures and levels of sweetness that we do not have to venture into the dubious world of chemical sweeteners.

Mini-Chat Point

Native Americans used maple sugar, pine sugar and agave nectar long, long ago to sweeten their foods. When you're not feeling bitter, salty or sour, try one of nature's many sugars and leave the chemicals in the lab.

 Above and Beyond!

Visit **www.sweetsavvy.com** for a comprehensive view into the world of all things sweet with recipes that make new sweeteners to your palate even more appealing. Have another taste test with natural sweeteners no one has ever tried before. Sweet!

Take Me Out to the Ballgame

• Seventh inning snack attack •

Ingredients

2 bags popping corn, each 4 ounces (113g)
2 cups (674g) molasses
1½ cups (300g) sugar
4 tablespoons (57g) butter
2 teaspoons (10ml) vanilla
2 cookie sheets
Spatula
Small pot

Directions

1. Pop corn per instructions.

2. Combine molasses, sugar and butter in the pot.

3. Bring to a boil and stir constantly, allowing one minute of boiling time.

4. Add vanilla and stir to blend.

5. Divide popcorn evenly on two cookie sheets.

6. Pour molasses mixture over popcorn.

7. Keep popcorn mixture laying flat on cookie sheet for 30 minutes or form into balls, wetting hands intermittently to keep the mixture from sticking to your hands.

8. Using a spatula, pull up popcorn and place in game-ready packaging such as saved cereal boxes with their inside wrapper or a spunky bandana.

Chat Point

Molasses is considered to have a significant amount of vitamins and minerals making it a nutritional sweetener choice. A lower grade of molasses is being analyzed and used in the country of Australia as part of their alternative fuels program.

Mini-Chat Point

You'll find molasses in most gingerbread recipes (yum) and in a dessert that is featured in songs and found among the Pennsylvania Dutch community — shoofly pie.

 Above and Beyond!

For diverse organic sweetener recipes, and comments from featured chefs who will be familiar to you, visit **www.organicsyrups.biz** and click on Wholesome Sweeteners. Baseball fans can check out **www.mlb.com**, search for "carbon neutral" and find the commendable green initiatives that have been put into play.

The Next Thing in Cooking Shows

• Featuring Jersey tomatoes •

Materials

Video camera
Friends, parents, siblings
Menu of locally grown, organic food choices

Directions

1. Plan your menu and have all ingredients and utensils on hand for one dish at a time.

2. Assign the videographer, chef and assistant roles.

3. Roll tape as chef and assistants prepare and talk to the camera about the locally grown organic food origins and benefits while putting together one dish at a time.

4. Clean the kitchen between each preparation segment.

5. Send your clip to friends and family and invite them to continue the trend wherever they are located.

Chat Point

Home videos will never be the same again once you have put the time and initiative into making your own cooking show segment. Encourage use of cloth napkins and mention that paper plates are not welcome in the sustainable kitchen.

Mini-Chat Point

Your food tastes better when you know what's in it and where it came from. Stir it up with your part in the cooking show and add a cup of enthusiasm to your role.

Above and Beyond!

Go to www.greenhome.com and click on Kitchen to find everything from bamboo chopping boards to reusable stainless steel food containers. Go on a food adventure at www.100milediet.org and follow the experience of Alisa Smith and J.B. MacKinnon's one-year experiment in local eating.

Toast of the Town

Ingredients

Day-young bread loaf
Glass of milk
Cookie cutters of choice
Cookie sheet
New small-size art paintbrush
Nonstick spray oil

Directions

1. Preheat oven to 350°F (176°C).

2. Spray the cookie sheet with a light coating of oil.

3. Place as many slices of bread as you can fit onto the cookie sheet.

4. Press cookie cutters into bread, without cutting through all the way.

5. Rinse the new paintbrush in water and pat dry.

6. Dip into your glass of milk and begin painting on each slice of bread, free-hand or within the outline of the cookie cutters.

7. Toast flat and watch through the lit window to see your milk paint become puffy and rise, bringing your picture or message to life.

Chat Point

Find rBGH-free milk in your grocery store and learn why it's a better choice. Organic bread is made from grain grown without use of pesticide, fungicide or herbicide. You wouldn't order that trio for breakfast if you had a choice, so choose organic.

 ### Mini-Chat Point

Organic means no added chemicals. Flour, water and salt sound like good friends but pesticide, fungicide and herbicide don't sound very nice and shouldn't be invited to the party.

 ### Above and Beyond!

Visit **www.sustainabletable.org** and click on Tools You Can Use. You will find the rBGH-Free Campaign with an educational page as well as a download capability to PDA or cell phone for a list of rBGH-free items.

Vegetable Mandala

• How does your garden grow? •

Ingredients

Colorful assortment of vegetables
Cutting board
Knife
Large round platter or plate

Directions

1. Wash and dry vegetables.

2. Cut into small pieces, some can even be teeny-tiny.

3. Arrange in a geometric pattern of your choosing, going around and around the plate.

4. Admire and serve with your favorite dip on the side.

Chat Point

Mandalas represent the whole universe in a geometric pattern with a complex history, often involving sand. This vegetable version is meant to inspire us, the whole universe, to focus more on the low end of the food chain where healthy vegetables thrive.

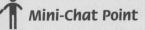

Mini-Chat Point

Veggies are nature's perfect fast-food even though they don't have musical commercials to make them look better. Find some favorites and experiment often with new ones.

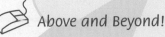 **Above and Beyond!**

The revitalized trend of growing your own vegetables is going strong. Join the fun and get your expert advice from www.organicgardening.com. With its unpredictable roller coaster of challenges and rewards, gardening requires the ability to laugh at oneself along the way and this site will help you do so — www.gardenhumor.com.

Happy Birthday Planet Earth

Ingredients

Serves 4

6" (15cm) soufflé dish (If more than one soufflé dish or
 suitable round pan is available, double the recipe to
 make two layers.)
1 cup (124g) grated zucchini
6 eggs
¾ cup (170g) ricotta cheese
3 tablespoons (15g) grated Parmesan cheese
2 tablespoons (2g) cilantro, chopped *optional*
Spray oil
Knife

Frosting

2 cups (420g) mashed potatoes

Directions

1. Preheat oven to 375°F (191°C).

2. Beat eggs in a large mixing bowl.

3. Add remaining ingredients and stir until smooth.

4. Spray soufflé dish with oil.

5. Pour mixture into soufflé dish and bake for 25
 minutes, until center is firm.

6. Cool for 10 minutes.

7. Meanwhile, prepare mashed potatoes and set
 aside.

8. Scrape side of soufflé dish with knife and invert
 frittata onto serving plate.

9. To frost, spread mashed potatoes evenly over first
 layer.

10. If you made a second layer, add on top of mashed
 potatoes.

11. Cover second layer with remaining mashed
 potatoes.

Chat Point

If zucchini does not grow near you,
experiment with another locally grown
vegetable. Farmer's markets are the best
option for locally grown potatoes. And if you
inquire, a farmer may give you a seed potato
so you can sprout one at home.

Mini-Chat Point

Birthday cake for dinner is beyond great!
Celebrate with candles and promise to take
care of the earth for another year.

Above and Beyond!

Counties, states and countries all have their respective farmer's market sites that you can visit. Checking into
www.ediblecommunities.com will point you to a food adventure of whole new proportions when you find the
one that serves your area. Click on Map; if there isn't one serving you, there is a link for you to start your own.

No More Plastic Smiles

• *Stop the advance of the cake toppers!* •

Ingredients

Carrot cake mix or similar product
Search cake mixes at **www.simplyorganicfoods.com**
and be tempted by their delicious Chai Spice Scone Mix
Decorations: party decoratifs, buttercream frosting,
candied flowers (**www.indiatree.com**)

Directions

1. Prepare cake mix according to package directions.

2. Bring out the artist in you by composing a unique
   cake topping without fake colors, fake flavors, or
   fake decorations — fake, fake, fake.

Chat Point

Little bits of plastic wind up in birds' stomachs like the turkey vulture. Bride and groom cake toppers often look like divorced couples and are a waste of money and an unnecessary use of plastic. When making or buying cakes, leave the plastic smiles for the world of harmless emoticons.

Mini-Chat Point

Next time it's Father's Day, tell Dad he's number one and give him a big hug. Make sure he knows what you didn't get for him on top of his cake.

 Above and Beyond! ————————————

Check **www.lifewithoutplastic.com** for all sorts of sustainable substitutes.

Chocolate Leaves

Ingredients

24 non-poisonous leaves such as camellia or rose
  leaves (without holes and well-shaped)
6 ounces (170g) semisweet chocolate chips
Unbleached wax paper or parchment paper
Baking sheet
Double boiler
Pastry brush

Directions

1. Wash and pat leaves dry.

2. Line baking sheet with wax or parchment paper

3. Melt the chocolate in the top of double boiler.

4. With pastry brush, spread melted chocolate over
   underside of leaves to get the best vein impressions
   on the chocolate.

5. Place leaves, chocolate side up, on the lined baking
   sheet.

6. Refrigerate until firm.

7. Use as a garnish with or without the actual leaf
   removed.

8. To remove leaf, hold stem and pull gently as
   chocolate and leaf will separate.

9. Arrange on top of an ice cream bowl, on a special
   cake or serve with dried fruits and nuts.

10. Even broken leaves will look attractive in pieces, as
    the vein pattern will still be evident.

11. Freeze for future use.

Chat Point

This is an attractive way to dress up kitchen
productions without entering the world
of plastic icing tips, artificial flavor, colored
frostings and sprinkles.

Mini-Chat Point

Leaves are not meant for eating unless you're
a giraffe, but chocolate ones are always fun
to eat. To make sure that the farmers who
grow the cocoa beans for your chocolate get
paid enough for their family to live, buy fair
trade chocolate.

Above and Beyond!

Check into **www.globalexchange.org**, click on Fair Trade and find ways to join the Fair Trade Cocoa Campaign.

Fair Trade
Organic
Chocolate
Coffee Cake

MAYA GOLD™

Ingredients

Serves 12

3.5 ounce (99g) Green & Black's Maya Gold chocolate
  bar, chopped (or similar product)
¼ pound (113g) butter, softened
8 ounces (227g) cream cheese, softened
1¼ cups (284g) sugar
2 eggs
1 teaspoon (5ml) vanilla extract
2 cups (454g) flour
1 teaspoon (3g) baking powder
½ teaspoon (1.5g) baking soda
¼ cup (60ml) cold milk
Mixing bowl
Mixer
Spray oil
Springform cake pan

Topping

¼ cup (57g) sugar
1 teaspoon (3g) cinnamon

Directions

1. Preheat oven to 350°F (177°C).

2. Spray springform pan on bottom and sides.

3. In a mixing bowl, cream butter, cream cheese and sugar.

4. Add eggs, vanilla extract, flour, baking powder and baking soda.

5. Mix until well combined.

6. Stir in cold milk and chopped chocolate bar.

7. Pour mixture into pan.

8. Combine topping ingredients and sprinkle over cake batter.

9. Bake for 1 hour.

Chat Point

Second-guess your chocolate purchases for fair trade certification and sustainable cultivation of cocoa. Life is like a box of chocolates and the more you know about fair trade, the more pleasant your bites will be.

Mini-Chat Point

Read your chocolate labels and make sure it sounds tasty and fair.

Above and Beyond!

In the U.S., Canada and the U.K. respectively, check into these sites featuring full fair trade information at **www.transfairusa.org**, **www.transfair.ca** and **www.fairtrade.org.uk**.

• Less palm oil, for peat's sake •

Ingredients

2 cucumbers
2 green peppers
Bowl large enough to submerge cucumbers in water
Sharp paring knife
Favorite dip

Directions

1. Cut both ends off cucumbers to make them flat on both ends.

2. Using paring knife, cut ½" (13mm) long thin slits into entire length of cucumbers.

3. Set aside into bowl filled with water which helps open up the slits.

4. Remove stemmed tops only from the green peppers; clean and core.

5. Cut peppers into four sections keeping bottoms intact.

6. To resemble palm leaves, keep all parts of the green pepper attached except for slicing the leaf pattern into the peppers.

7. Remove cucumbers from water bowl and pat dry.

8. Stand cucumbers on end and place peppers on top.

9. Serve with favorite dip.

Chat Point

The palm tree in its native setting has many uses and is the source of roofing, food and trade. However, the increased use of palm oil in everything from margarine to shampoo has brought about widespread burning of peat lands. Logging of rainforests is occurring to make room for palm tree plantations. Eliminating palm oil from the food chain is nearly impossible, but supporting companies that use palm oil derived through sustainable practices is doable.

Mini-Chat Point

If you use anything too much, it gets shabby or breaks, like your favorite stuffed animal. The peat lands and rainforests are broken now from getting used too much.

Above and Beyond!

Visit www.spectrumorganics.com and search "palm oil" to learn more about sustainable palm oil. At www.adventureservicetourism.com, click on Palm Tree Conservation and find a new destination for your tourist dollars.

Quesadilla Snowflakes

• No two alike •

Ingredients

12-ounce (340g) package soft round quesadillas
8 ounces (114g) cream cheese, softened to room
  temperature
¼ cup (50g) white sugar
½ teaspoon (1.2g) cinnamon
Butter knife
Clean scissors

Directions

1. Fold a quesadilla into quarters.

2. Using clean scissors, snip away as you would a
   paper snowflake.

3. Gently spread cream cheese on the quesadilla,
   taking care not to rip the design.

4. Combine cinnamon and sugar and sprinkle over
   quesadilla with a teaspoon.

5. Lift up quesadilla to see stencil pattern from freshly
   cut snowflake.

6. Fold back into quarters and enjoy!

Chat Point

Make every effort to stop global warming
and preserve the fun and beauty of
snowflakes. One way to help slow global
warming trends is by turning off the
computer, printer and TV when the night is
over. Make it a habit.

Mini-Chat Point

Say good-bye to the ghost of "phantom load."
Play hide-and-seek in the dark to see how
many things you can find that are still using
energy with their tiny lights still glowing.

Above and Beyond!

View www.whatsmyco2.com and click on Phantom Loads located on the left bar.

Solar Turkey-Melt Oven

Ingredients

2 English muffins sliced in half
4 slices turkey
4 slices cheese
1 large shoe box
1 Popsicle stick
Aluminum foil
3 sheets black construction paper

Directions

1. Cover inside lid of box with aluminum foil.

2. Cover inside of box bottom with black construction paper.

3. Place English muffin halves in shoe box, cut side up.

4. Layer turkey and cheese on top of each English muffin.

5. Prop open lid with Popsicle stick to create a 45-degree angle.

6. Point towards the sun on a windowsill or in a yard.

7. Heat will reflect off the aluminum foil and be absorbed by the black paper layer on the bottom creating enough heat to melt the cheese.

8. Traditional homemade box solar ovens can heat up to 275°F (135°C). They require a plastic wrap layer which we avoided in this version.

Chat Point

Catch some rays and put them to work for you. A simple set of solar ovens can be waiting for the next set of kids to arrive at your house. Melt chocolate for s'mores or cheese for English muffin pizza to expand your solar oven kitchen cuisine.

Mini-Chat Point

Nothing is s'more delicious than saving energy while making fun snacks.

Above and Beyond!

For the real thing, take a look at a more advanced solar oven at **www.solarcooking.org/plans**.

Geodesic Dome

Materials

1 box of toothpicks
1 container of organic jelly candies or organic
  gummi bears

Directions

1. Count out five gummies and five toothpicks.

2. Join five gummies with the five toothpicks to form
   a five-sided polygon as the base of the dome.

3. Build upward, forming triangles and attaching
   gummies as you work up and around.

Chat Point

Buckminster Fuller's design has reached
across playgrounds everywhere, the Epcot
Center in Walt Disney World®, and beyond. Its
triangular segments are super strong and its
bubble shape allows for less energy use than
any other shelter system.

Mini-Chat Point

Can you guess why this famous dome uses
less energy than a same-size house? It is
because there are no walls and no roof, so
the warm air or the cool air can flow more
evenly. Warm or cool air in a typical house
bumps into a wall or goes to the top and
stays there…so you need more.

Above and Beyond!

Visit **www.edwardandsons.com** for organic gummies of the cutest and tastiest kind and make all kinds of
structures with the triangular support system. Visit **www.bfi.org** and look under Image Galleries to see the many
applications of the geodesic dome.

Coconut Macaroons

Ingredients

Yields approx. 36 macaroons
3 egg whites
1 cup (227g) sugar
1 cup (227g) shredded coconut
½ cup (113g) semisweet chocolate chips
Parchment paper
Spray oil
Cookie sheet
Large coconut shavings for garnish *optional*
Double boiler or saucepan

Directions

1. Preheat oven to 300°F (149°C).

2. Beat egg whites until frothy.

3. Add sugar and continue beating until glossy.

4. Fold in coconut.

5. Spray cookie sheet with oil.

6. Drop mixture by spoonfuls onto the cookie sheet.

7. Bake for 25 to 30 minutes until lightly browned.

8. Cool for 15 minutes and then remove with a spatula.

9. Melt chocolate in top of double boiler.

10. Have a sheet of parchment paper ready on countertop.

11. Carefully dip cooled macaroons, bottom end only, into melted chocolate.

12. Place on parchment paper for setting before serving. Garnish with coconut shavings if desired.

Chat Point

The coconut tree is one of the most useful trees sustainably grown and harvested. In warmer climates, the fronds are used for making roofs, the wood is used for building, the heart of palm and the nut are edible and the outer husk of coconuts is used for bed stuffing and mulch.

Mini-Chat Point

Did you know that the coconut is the largest seed in the world?

Above and Beyond!

Take a look at www.newbalance.com and search for "CoCoNa" to learn about the coconut's contribution to CoCoNa's™ apparel technology.

Monkey
Business
Trail Mix

• Only flying monkeys should be homeless •

Ingredients

2 cups (454g) banana chips
1 cup (74g) coconut flakes or chips
1 cup (125g) walnut pieces
1 cup (168g) semisweet chocolate chips

Directions

1. Combine all ingredients in bowl.

2. Add a ladle and scoop into eager hands.

Chat Point

The rainforest is vital in so many ways and consumer behavior can help preservation and recovery efforts. Check out **www.secondnaturecd.com** and click on Rainforest Alliance for screensavers and desktop wallpaper. Second Nature supports and contributes to numerous nonprofit environmental organizations.

Mini-Chat Point

Stop monkeying around and share your monkey mix with friends. While you're munching, look up "howler monkeys," "black-capped capuchins" and "squirrel monkeys." They all live in the rainforest and the more you know, the more you'll be able to help them and the rainforest.

Above and Beyond!

The Rainforest Alliance has tremendous resources and research available on their Web site about rainforest preservation and the value of our informed consumer purchasing power. Visit **www.rainforest-alliance.org**.

Not the Only Pebble on the Beach

Ingredients

Serves 4

6 graham crackers
2 hardboiled eggs
2 fruit leathers
4 toothpicks
1 or 2 bottle caps
Kashi Mighty Bites™ or similar cereal in fun shapes
Beach décor from around the house
Chocolate vermicelli or similar chocolate sprinkles
 (www.indiatree.com)
Rolling pin
Cutting board
Blue dish, tray or plate for water effect

Directions

1. Prepare sandy beach by crushing graham crackers, one at a time, with rolling pin on a cutting board.

2. Slice eggs in half lengthwise to form boat hulls.

3. Cut fruit leather in half across width.

4. Using toothpicks, create sails by poking through the fruit leather from top to bottom.

5. Place sails upright in the egg boat hulls.

6. Set beach scene on a blue dish, plate or tray by arranging the graham cracker sand, a few ants courtesy of India Tree's chocolate vermicelli (sprinkles), Kashi Mighty Bites beach-goers and an offensive piece of trash in the form of bottle caps on one side.

7. On the water side, set up sailboats to complete the beach scene, adding any beach décor you have on hand.

Chat Point

Beaches have been barometers of what's floating in the water when it washes up to shore. **www.beachcleanup.org** is an example of successful adopt-a-beach, 30-minute clean-up programs that can be adapted to your waterway anywhere.

Mini-Chat Point

When you go to the beach, the last thing you want to dig up with your sand shovel is garbage. Remember to carry your trash off the beach to keep it beautifully clean.

Save Our Natural Resources

Above and Beyond!

The swirling mass of plastic debris in the north Pacific Ocean should be enough to have us all pass up plastic purchases whenever possible. Visit **www.greatgarbagepatch.org**.

Sunflower Gelato Cake

Ingredients

Serves 12

2 pints (907g) mango gelato or other naturally yellow
  gelato or sorbet
1 pint (454g) chocolate gelato or sorbet
1 cup (168g) chocolate chips
Large serving platter and several small plates
Large flat spoon
Butter knife
Fork
Sunflower petals for garnish *optional*

Directions

1. Allow all three gelato containers to slightly soften.

2. Scoop half of the chocolate gelato and shape into a
   ball in the middle of the serving platter.

3. Pat down to flatten maintaining a nice circular
   shape to form center of sunflower.

4. Press chocolate chips into the softened sunflower
   center to serve as seeds.

5. Return serving platter to freezer.

6. Using a small plate, scoop out small amounts of the
   mango gelato and shape into simple flower petals
   with a butter knife.

7. Slide fork under individual petals and place onto
   another small plate that can be moved into the
   freezer to maintain shape until ready to assemble.

8. Continue shaping, moving and freezing until all
   sorbet has been used.

9. Remove serving platter from freezer and work
   with one plate of petals at a time to layer around
   the sunflower center until complete. Garnish with
   petals if desired.

Chat Point

The sunflower often is used by worldwide
organizations that advocate for a healthy
environment. Blackwell's organic gelatos
and sorbets make a delicious version of this
environmentally conscious symbol.

Mini-Chat Point

The sunflower has a beautiful face waiting
for little fingers and tiny beaks to pick its
seeds. It has another use too, being grown for
sunflower oil to be used in salad dressings,
mayonnaise and some soaps.

Above and Beyond!

Gather some insight into the value of delicious organic products when you visit **www.blackwellsorganic.com**
and click on the About Us section.

Phased by the Moon

Sugar Cookie Dough Ingredients

Yields approx. 36 cookies
¾ cup (90g) powdered sugar
½ cup (114g) butter, softened
1 egg
1 teaspoon (5ml) vanilla extract
1¼ cups (171g) all-purpose flour
1 teaspoon (5g) baking soda
Rolling pin
Cookie sheet
Drinking glass
Flour for working surface
Butter knife
Large glasses of milk at serving time
Nonstick cooking spray

Frosting Ingredients

1 cup (168g) white chocolate chips
¼ cup (60ml) milk
¼ cup (57g) butter cut in small bits
Small saucepan
Mixing bowl
Butter knife

Directions

1. Mix powdered sugar, butter, egg and vanilla until well blended.

2. Add flour and baking soda and mix well.

3. Cover and refrigerate for 2 hours.

Chat Point

Set a plate with five to six cookies each, accompanied by the requisite glass of milk. Bite cookies, gently and evenly, to form the phases of the moon.

Mini-Chat Point

Can you always see the moon? Sometimes, it's just a cloudy day, but depending on where you live, pollution also can be hiding the moon.

4. Make frosting by combining all ingredients in a small saucepan, stirring on low heat until smooth and melted. Pour into bowl and refrigerate until ready to use.

5. Preheat oven to 375°F (190°C).

6. Turn dough out onto a floured countertop and divide in half.

7. Roll each half until thin.

8. Dip open end of drinking glass in flour and then cut dough into circle shapes.

9. Place about 1" (25mm) apart on sprayed cookie sheet.

10. Bake for 10 minutes and cool before removing from cookie sheet.

11. Once completely cool, spread frosting with butter knife.

Above and Beyond!

Visit **www.worldcarfree.net** and organize your town, block or city to join the blissful day without cars and their pollution every September 22.

Something's Fishy

• Wild thing •

Ingredients

Yields 8 salmon cakes
4 cups (907g) cooked wild Alaskan salmon pieces
1 cup (108g) bread crumbs
4 eggs
Olive oil
1 teaspoon (6g) sea salt
Plate with additional bread crumbs for coating
Skillet

Directions

1. Pour olive oil to coat the bottom of a skillet and turn heat to low.

2. Beat eggs with sea salt.

3. Add salmon and bread crumbs. Stir to blend.

4. Form into 1" (25mm) thick cakes using your hands to shape.

5. Coat each cake with bread crumbs, top and bottom.

6. Place cakes into warmed skillet and fry until golden brown on each side.

Chat Point

Learning about fishery practices around the world gives everyone insight into making minimal-mercury, sustainable fish choices.

Mini-Chat Point

By making the right fish choices when we buy and eat them, we can make sure that we don't just have plastic fish left.

Above and Beyond!

Visit the Seafood Watch Program at **www.mbayaq.org** and find a most useful pocket guide for making fish choices. Under the Save the Oceans tab, click on Seafood Watch.

Spouting Off

Ingredients

1 watermelon
Assorted fruit such as grapes, melon balls, berries
Dried flower sprig
Sharp paring knife
Melon baller
White-colored pencil

Directions

1. Using the white-colored pencil, draw a whale outline on top of watermelon including a tail.

2. With sharp paring knife, cut away shell in pieces as you go, holding to your outline.

3. As in pumpkin carving, create eyes, leaving the vine end of the watermelon to serve as the nose.

4. Carve a mouth without cutting through to the fruit so juice from the fruit won't escape through the mouth.

5. Scoop out watermelon with a melon baller.

6. Add assorted fruits in combination with the watermelon and heap up nicely in the whale watermelon.

7. Above the eyes, poke a small hole with the sharp paring knife and push in dried flower sprig as if coming out of the blowhole.

Chat Point

Whales live in a changing environment with many man-made perils ranging from whaling to habitat destruction.

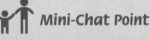

Mini-Chat Point

For an ongoing dialogue about protecting the whale, see if the Sand Play Set from **www.greentoys.com** is right for your little one. Every time you play with someone else, there is a chance to mention these earth-friendly toys made from recycled milk jugs so we can all play next to the whales for a long time.

Above and Beyond!

Visit **www.whaleresearch.com** and take a look at Orca Cam™ for a real life whale experience.

Edible Chain Reaction

• Domino effect •

Ingredients

1 box of graham crackers

12-ounce (340g) jar of peanut butter or 8-ounce (227g) package of cream cheese

1 playing set of dominoes

Assortment of raisins, dried cranberries and chocolate chips

Directions

1. Crack graham cracker sections into rectangles.

2. Spread with a thin, smooth layer of peanut butter, cream cheese or both.

3. Line up a full set of numbered dominoes to have one of each stone represented as a guide.

4. Using raisins, dried cranberries and chocolate chips, make your own edible set of dominoes.

5. Play several rounds before eating.

Chat Point

Have a conversation about every good sustainable living element that you practice having a domino effect. Someone notices that you carpool. A friend asks why you save all the school notices next to your printer. Work colleagues make fun of you turning off your PC during your lunch hour or for lengthy meetings, but they also want to know why.

Mini-Chat Point

Line up all the dominoes and tip one to start the toppling domino effect. What's your domino effect? Did you give your outgrown clothes to a smaller friend? Do you dry your clothes on a line in your backyard or even your bedroom (makes great hiding places)?

Above and Beyond!

Domino No.1 — Don't let your car idle.

Domino No. 2 — Wear a sweater.

Domino No. 3 — Vacuum the coils in the back of your refrigerator.

You have just started three new games. For more great sustainable living ideas, visit www.idealbite.com and sign up for their daily tips.

From Darkness Comes Light

• Green is the new black •

Black and Green Snack Menu Ingredients

Green: asparagus, zucchini, organic raw pepitas (www.wholefoodsmarket.com)

Black: mushrooms (www.wholefoodsmarket.com), wild rice (www.lundberg.com), dark organic 85% chocolate bar (www.greenandblacks.com)
Serving bowls

Directions

1. Steam and serve asparagus, zucchini and mushrooms.

Chat Point

Black limes are a Middle Eastern spice used to flavor stews and pots of beans. Prick holes in the whole lime or cut in half and add to a simmering pot. They start out as regular green limes, are boiled in salt water for a length of time and then sun dried to reach their spicy state while maintaining their citrus kick — the ultimate combination of green and black.

Mini-Chat Point

Black has always been a big part of the "classic" wardrobe. It is the color of magic. Now, the color green and what it stands for is making its own splash and everything is coming up green.

2. Prepare wild rice according to package directions.

3. Break apart chocolate bar and share.

Black and Green Dinner Menu Ingredients

Black sesame tahini
   (www.livingtreecommunity.com)
Green beans
Whole grain black rice a.k.a. "nobleman's rice"
   (www.formaggiokitchen.com)
Green cucumbers
Black beans
Green shelled pistachios
Black limes (www.nirmalaskitchen.com)
Black and white kettle corn (www.lesserevil.com)
Olive oil
Knife
Serving bowls, platter

Directions

1. Prepare rice and black beans according to package directions.

2. Steam green beans and set aside.

3. Wash and slice cucumber into lengthwise slices for dipping in tahini.

4. Pour pistachios into a serving bowl

5. Scoop tahini into a serving bowl, stirring in a small amount of olive oil to achieve desired consistency.

6. Set out black limes on serving plate as conversation piece to be used for a later meal. (See Chat Point for what to say about these unique limes.)

7. Share kettle corn.

Above and Beyond!

See what you can find that's cool, green and useful at **www.gaiam.com**.

King Cake Surprise

Ingredients

Serves 10
Organic vanilla or lemon cake mix (**www.oetker.us**)
1 teaspoon (2g) cinnamon
Organic vanilla icing mix (**www.oetker.us**)
Bundt pan
Small tape measure
Butter knife
Mardi Gras decorations
Decorating or sparkling sugars in sunflower yellow
 and emerald city green (**www.indiatree.com**)

Directions

Organic cake and frosting mixes are available in many
health food stores and online.

1. Prepare cake batter according to package
   directions. Stir in cinnamon.

2. Halfway through baking time, remove from oven
   and add the small tape measure.

3. Return to oven and continue baking.

4. Mix icing according to package directions.

5. Allow cake to fully cool.

6. Spread icing over cake and generously sprinkle
   with decorating sugars.

7. Add Mardi Gras decorations and serve

Chat Point

Mardi Gras King Cake usually will surprise one
lucky cake eater who discovers a small plastic
baby. Rather than biting the baby, the tape
measure will be the mystery to find. Whoever
has the tape measure in their piece of cake
gives a verbal account of how they measure up
in following sustainable living practices. Per the
tradition, the measuring tape recipient will have
to make a King Cake for the next gathering.

Mini-Chat Point

If you didn't get the measuring tape on your
plate, you can ask questions of the person
who did, such as do you visit the local library
often? Did you get your name off junk mail
lists? Do you have funny looking light bulbs
in your house? Or, do you have pet worms
under your sink or in your backyard?

Above and Beyond!

Look at **www.earthday.net** and search for "ecological footprint calculator" to get a good read on your habits and
where you can improve.

Look Who's Coming to Dinner

Locavore

• Celebrity dish •

Ingredients

Vegetarian cookbooks from the library
Locally grown ingredients
Phantom guest

Directions

1. Plan a vegetarian menu with some selections you have never tried before.

2. Purchase and prepare.

3. Name your dinner after a vegetarian celebrity of choice such as The Daryl Hannah Mexicana or The Chris Martin Spartan.

Chat Point

Pledge to eat a vegetarian meal at least once a week to reduce the tremendous carbon footprint surrounding the production of meat. Food choices greatly impact the planet, and when it comes to meat, less is more. To be informed on more in-depth animal issues, visit **www.farmsanctuary.org**. Since there are supposedly over 50,000 edible plants on this earth, salad should be what's super-sized!

Mini-Chat Point

What does vegetarian mean? A person who does not eat meat or fish.

What does vegan mean? A person who does not eat any animal or dairy products.

Above and Beyond!

Check into **www.happycow.net** for a global directory of vegetarian restaurants and health food stores located near you.

Rice Pudding
Comfort Food

• Like white on rice •

Ingredients

Serves 6

1 cup (174g) rice cooked according to package directions

½ cup (100g) sugar

2 tablespoons (16g) cornstarch

4 eggs yolks (egg whites may be frozen for other use)

6 cups (1,440ml) half-and-half (mix of 50% whole milk and 50% cream)

½ vanilla bean pod

Cinnamon

Hot water in a teakettle

2 casserole pans, one should fit inside a larger one

Directions

1. Preheat oven to 350°F (177°C).

2. Cut vanilla bean pod in half and scrape tiny seeds into large mixing bowl.

3. Add sugar, cornstarch and egg yolks and mix well.

4. Pour in half-and-half.

5. Fold in cooked rice.

6. Turn mixture into smaller casserole pan and place inside larger one.

7. Carefully pour hot water into larger one creating a 1" (25mm) bath.

8. Bake for 1½ hours.

9. Upon removing from oven, sprinkle with cinnamon and serve warm.

Chat Point

Lundberg Family Farms operates a sustainable agriculture rice paddy. They rotate crops with clover and beans, let the field sit empty for a couple of years and encourage ducks to roam and naturally fertilize the field before they grow another crop of organic rice.

Mini-Chat Point

Did you know that brown and white rice can grow on the same plant?

 Above and Beyond!

Visit **www.lundberg.com**, click on Farming and learn more about sustainable rice farming. To share rice with others, play **www.freerice.com** and walk away with an expanded vocabulary to boot.

Sustainable Living Web Sites

w.poopoopaper.com
ement of change: you

www.loop.ph
element of change: y

uncommongoods.com
of change: you

www.reestore.c
lucky element of change: yo

venturi.fr
of change: you

www.nigelsecostore
ky element of change: you

.aurorarobson.com
element of change: you

Ingredients

1 box of fortune cookies
Paper and pencil or computer and printing paper
List of innovative green Web sites to share with friends
 and family

Directions

1. Hand write or computer print additional fortunes to
   be slipped inside fortune cookies.

2. Surf the Web together.

Chat Point

Check out these Web sites:
• www.poopoopaper.com
• www.nigelsecostore.com
• www.reestore.com
• www.loop.ph
• www.venturi.fr
• www.uncommongoods.com
• www.aurorarobson.com

Mini-Chat Point

For fun online games and coloring printables,
visit **www.ecokids.ca.**

Above and Beyond!

Support your favorite sustainable living product or art piece by introducing it to a store near you. Check out
www.hubcapcreatures.com.

Ingredients

Yields approx 36 cookies

1½ cups (180g) powdered sugar
1 cup (227g) rBGH-free butter, softened
1 egg
1 teaspoon (5ml) vanilla
1¼ cups (156g) all-purpose or whole-wheat flour
1 teaspoon (5g) baking soda
Mixing bowl
Beater
Rolling pin
Cookie sheet
Nonstick spray
Seaside summer cookie cutters or footprint cookie
  cutter (**www.kingarthurflour.com**)
Decorations without chemicals (**www.indiatree.com**)

Directions

1. Mix sugar, butter, egg and vanilla together in the mixing bowl.

2. Add flour and baking soda. Mix.

3. Cover dough and place in fridge for at least two hours.

4. Preheat oven to 375°F (190°C).

5. Break cold dough into smaller sections and roll out on a flour-sprinkled countertop to approximately ¼" (6mm) thickness.

6. Using the footprint cookie cutter, cut into footprint shapes and place onto lightly sprayed cookie sheet without touching neighboring cookies.

7. Bake for 7 to 8 minutes until golden.

8. Remove from cookie sheet and cool completely before decorating.

9. "Paint" the toenails; add a pinky ring; be creative.

Chat Point

Examine what reducing your carbon footprint really means. The overall concept is to think about how much electricity a product uses from beginning to end. For example, cold drinks have to be manufactured, packaged, kept cool in a truck or train car, shipped and displayed in an open-front store refrigerator case all before your first gulp. How much carbon dioxide and other greenhouse gases are used for each product before it reaches you?

Mini-Chat Point

Imagine your banana sitting with more bananas on an airplane seat next to you. That banana sure travels far to get to your fruit bowl. That's called "having a carbon footprint" and everything you use or eat has one.

 Above and Beyond!

Learn how to measure your shoe size in calculating your carbon footprint at **www.terrapass.com**.

The Kitchen Sink
COMPLETION CHART
(food projects)

You've Mastered It!

You've learned many new ways to live a sustainable life that you can share with those around you as any great chef enjoys sharing his creations. Color or note each grape after you complete the projects.

Master
Sustainable
Chef

Section 3: The Studio Gallery
(craft projects)

Whether it's engaging in the art of pointillism or dipping fingers in beet-infused finger paint, the sky is the limit to your creativity. Uncork new uses for the plentiful bottle stoppers and twist twigs into something radiant and useful. Give a second life to LPs and 45s and frame your favorite photos with last week's milk jug. Roll up your sleeves and dig into a field of objects that will inspire you beyond reduce, reuse and recycle.

Air Care

• Up in the air •

Materials

Cinnamon sticks
Medium-size beads
Jumbo paper clips
Essential oil (**www.auracacia.com**) *optional*

Directions

1. Open up the paper clip to be straight.

2. String a bead to the end of one paper clip and bend over in a loop to reinsert back into the bead, forming an end post.

3. Put the cinnamon stick over the paper clip.

4. Add another bead.

5. Loop end of paper clip into a hook to hang over a visor attachment in a car or a valance in a bedroom or bathroom.

6. For a longer version, instead of ending with a hook, loop paper clip through another paper clip loop and start on the second one in the same format.

7. Once cinnamon smell has evaporated, freshen it up by dabbing essential oil of choice onto the cinnamon sticks for another life.

Chat Point

Conventional air fresheners, in all shapes and sizes, carry a wave of chemicals into your breathing space, wafting on artificial scents mimicking everything from cookies to fruit. Instead, choose baking soda, lemons, real spices, simmering vanilla bean pods or cloves on the stove top or bake a real batch of homemade cookies and savor the smell as much as the taste.

Mini-Chat Point

For a tour through a virtual house, go to **www.epa.gov** and search for "learn about chemicals around your house." Be sure to visit the bathroom and click on the air freshener to find out what's really in it — yikes!

Above and Beyond!

Read about hazardous chemicals in places that may surprise you, including air fresheners, at **www.epa.gov**. Search for "chemicals in the household kids."

It is
My Beeswax

• Just say no…to paraffin •

Materials

Sheets of beeswax (At **www.magiccabin.com**, go to Product Finder and search for "beeswax." It's sweet-smelling, reusable, plant-dyed beeswax perfect for rolling into candles.)
Cotton wicking (included if ordering the set from Magic Cabin®)
Candleholders
Matches

Directions

1. Cut cotton wicking to the length of the beeswax plus 1" (25mm).

2. Place wicking on one side of the beeswax with the extra 1" (25mm) hanging over the edge.

3. Gently, very gently, start warming up the beeswax with careful rolling beginning on the wicking side of the beeswax and continuing to the end.

4. As the wax warms up through back and forth motions, it will be possible to roll it tighter into the desired circumference.

5. Experiment with birthday-candle sizes and keep them ready for many happy returns.

6. Form designs to push onto the outside of the candles for more decorative versions.

Chat Point

Paraffin candles made from petroleum byproducts produce toxic soot, are laden with synthetic fragrances and number a population size greater than some countries. Converting to beeswax candles makes perfect sense.

Mini-Chat Point

Support a bee colony and make natural candles that burn cleaner than all the rest.

Above and Beyond!

Learn more about the benefits of beeswax candles vs. petroleum-based candles by visiting **www.honeygardens.com** and click on Beeswax Candles. You'll be encouraged to purchase 100-percent beeswax candles. Current labeling may use the word beeswax but only contain 51-percent beeswax.

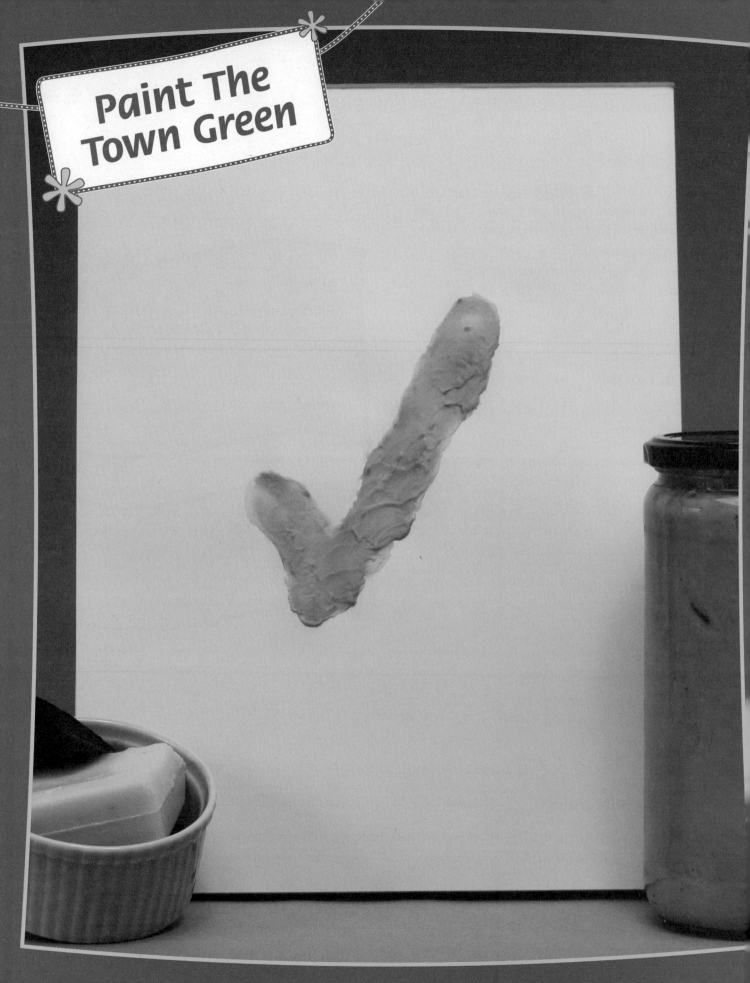

Paint The Town Green

• Zero VOC rocks •

Materials

1½ cups (192g) cornstarch
1 cup (240ml) colored water, selected and prepared
 from Color Key, page 7
⅔ cup (146g) grated soap (try 8-ounce olive and
 honey bar soap from www.kissmyface.com)
Recycled baby food jar with lid
Recycled cardboard or paper
Large-size pot
Stirring spoon

Directions

1. Melt grated soap and colored water in the pot.

2. Add cornstarch.

3. Stir over low heat until mixture begins to thicken.

4. Cool completely and spoon into recycled jar.

5. Dip fingers in paint, and go to town on cardboard or paper.

6. Mix new colors and combine others to make new ones.

7. Add water as needed to maintain consistency.

8. Store in refrigerator up to one week.

Chat Point

Air inside the house or office is considered more polluted than outside air several times over. Make sure paint choices are not contributing to the chemical load in favorite rooms. In addition to headaches, conventional paint continues to off-gas long after it dries.

Mini-Chat Point

If there are things that you can't pronounce in your finger paints, like toluene and ethylene glycol, leave them on the shelf. Soap flakes, cornstarch and colors from nature are not only more fun to put together, but very safe.

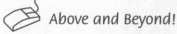 **Above and Beyond!**

For adult-size projects, zero VOC (volatile organic chemical) paint is available at Home Depot® from **www.freshairechoice.com**. In addition, check out the story behind the olive oil bars from **www.kissmyface.com** and discover how the company supports **www.wecansolveit.org**.

Tie-dye —Give it a Try

• No gloves required •

Materials

1 white organic cotton shirt or an existing white T-shirt from your closet
1 color from the Color Key, page 7, doubling the amount of water and pigment to accommodate a T-shirt bath (with the exception of green, all colors listed work well)
1 clean milk jug
8 to 10 rubber bands
Scissors

Directions

1. After preparing color bath using the instructions on page 7, allow to cool.

2. Using rubber bands, gather small fingerfuls of T-shirt fabric and wrap in rubber bands several times to tightly hold in place. Do this all over the T-shirt.

3. Cut spout off milk jug and stuff T-shirt into milk jug.

4. Pour color bath into milk jug to cover T-shirt.

5. Allow to soak for several hours.

6. Remove T-shirt and wring out with your hands (your hands will wash clean).

7. Hang to dry.

8. Remove rubber bands, releasing beautiful tie-dye markings.

9. Hand wash in cold water after first wearing, and then add to regular wash cycles.

Chat Point

How easy to make a tie-dye shirt without the packaging and chemical dyes of a kit. You can dive right in with your hands without consequence and the end result is attractive.

Mini-Chat Point

Nature is so colorful with different shades coming from nuts, fruits, flowers and leaves. Your shirt may even attract fruit flies. Say, "no thank you" to kits using chemical dyes when you can have more fun making your own from nature without using plastic gloves.

Above and Beyond!

There are mysteries about the true content of over-the-counter fabric dyes as the actual source of the pigment can remain undisclosed. But you can be sure that they do not sound as understandable and non-toxic as the food and spice versions offered in the Color Key on page 7. For more dying information, visit www.motherearthnews.com and search for "eggs and dyes."

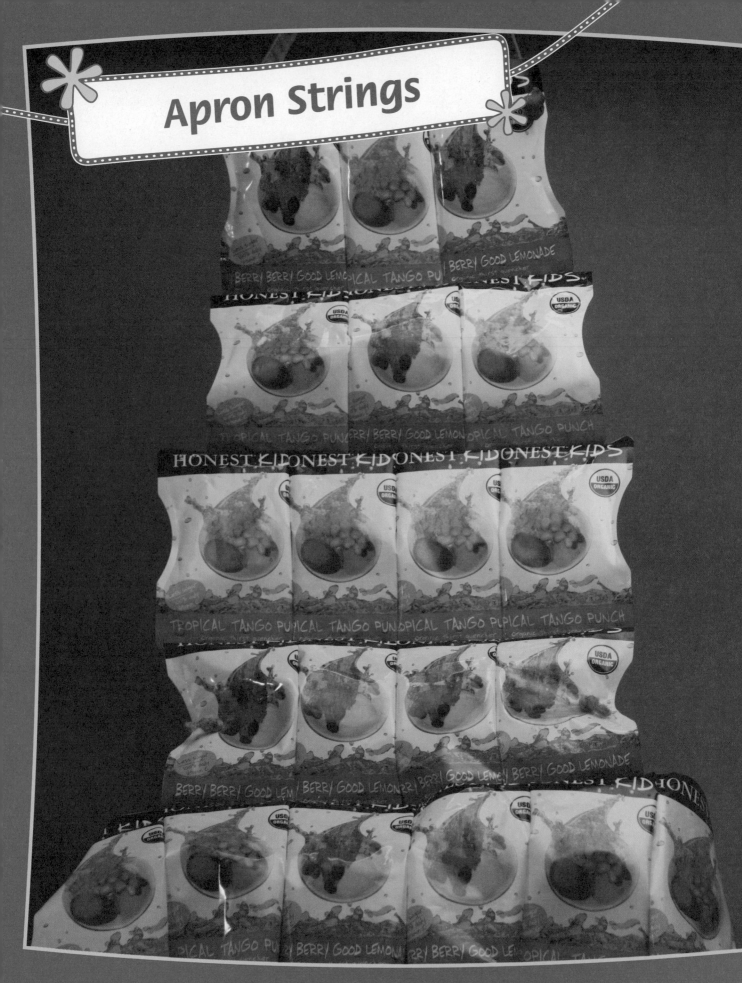

Materials

Lots and lots of empty Honest Tea® kids' drink
  pouches (or similar brand)
Measuring tape
Hole punch
Stapler
Twine
Scissors

Directions

1. Measure chest width of apron recipient and desired length of apron.

2. Line up measuring tape on a flat surface and fit the empty juice pouches across to see how many are needed for upper chest portion.

3. Plan on two to three rows for upper chest portion.

4. Add one on each end and continue downward until reaching desired length.

5. With colorful graphics side of juice pouches facedown, match up sides to form a seam line.

6. Staple in place and continue across and down to join up all juice pouches.

7. Punch holes in upper two corners of apron and one on each side where the waist will be.

8. Measure a loop of twine around the neck of the recipient and cut to size.

9. Tying a double knot on one end, string the twine through the hole on one corner and through the other corner and end with another double knot.

10. Measure two lengths of twine suitable for tying apron behind recipient's back.

11. Double-knot ends of both tie straps, thread through respective holes and double-knot the end.

Chat Point

Children's drink selections are loaded with high-fructose corn syrup, sugar and artificial colors. If you were mixing your own kids' drinks, you would never reach for the FDC #7 Red and call a neighbor for a cup of high-fructose corn syrup. Honest Tea is made from real ingredients and comes in three great flavors with only 10 grams of sugar in each pouch.

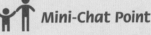 **Mini-Chat Point**

Be a label reader. Your juice actually should come from a fruit and not sound like a lab report.

Above and Beyond!

Visit www.honesttea.com and read an ingredient list you will understand. Find out about their "fair trade efforts" and "organic certification."

CSA stands for Community Supported Agriculture. This activity is a twist on the traditional geometrical tangram puzzle (Chinese puzzle).

Materials

One set of 10 cardboard tangram pieces (can be traced from a wooden set, cut out of cardboard or drawn freehand from an online search of tangram shapes.)

Directions

1. Write the following on each tangram shape:

   a. Freshest, local produce that has not seen the inside of a truck or rail car.

   b. Discover new fruits and vegetables that would not have been chosen in the supermarket aisle.

   c. Expand recipe base when a surplus of one harvested item arrives.

   d. Share a share if produce will be too much to use.

   e. Know a farm worker is being paid a fair wage in a CSA arrangement.

   f. Know where produce is coming from.

   g. Keep money in the community.

   h. Buy a share and contribute time.

   i. Community dinners will be remembered.

   j. Sign up now!

Chat Point

Each CSA-gram is a Chat Point to help you locate and support a CSA in your vicinity.

Mini-Chat Point

To play with CSA-grams, visit **www.pbskids.org** and search for "tangram game" to learn the fundamentals. Keep it in an envelope and take it to restaurants to play with friends while you wait.

 Above and Beyond!

Take a look at **www.sustainabletable.org**. Under Shop Sustainable click on CSA for a greater understanding of the sensibilities for supporting CSAs and finding one near you. For those in Canada and the U.K., ask at your local farmer's market. One located in Ontario, Canada is **www.eatlocalsudbury.com**.

Don't Throw the Towel Out Yet

• *A day at the beach* •

Materials

2 well-worn bath towels
Fabric scissors

Directions

1. Choose one bath towel that will have the outside seams removed, reserving the other one to be the main towel that will form the bag.

2. Cut all four seams off the towel.

3. This towel can be used for a pet blanket or cut into dishcloths.

4. Fold the main towel in half.

5. Without touching the fold line, make slits several inches (8cm) apart going up both sides from the fold line to the open top of the towel.

6. Be sure to cut through both towel layers to achieve these slits.

7. Continue across the open top of the towel by making slits but allowing a sizeable opening for the handles and for items as large as another towel to be placed inside the bag.

8. Tie a tight knot on one end of the longest seams cut from the other towel.

9. Thread cut-off seams through the slits of both towel layers in an over-and-under pattern to reach up both sides to the open end of the towel leaving a knot in each corner at the bottom fold.

10. Knot the top ends and cut.

11. Using one of the smaller cut-off seams, thread over-and-under leaving a knotted end at the corner of the open top of the bag and knotting again on the other corner.

12. Do the same with the other side of the open top of the bag.

13. In the middle of the open top of the bag, pull the slack of the towel seams up to form handles.

Chat Point

This beach pillowcase bag is great for days at the beach as you can stuff it with two usable bath towels. One beach towel is never enough and after a day of use, it's either too sandy, too wet or both. Keep one inside your beach pillowcase bag; use it as a pillow and when your day of fun is over, you'll have a perfectly dry, sand-free towel to use. Everything is washable so you can lather, rinse and repeat.

Mini-Chat Point

Pick your new beach towels carefully and ask for thick organic cotton choices so it will last as long as possible.

Above and Beyond!

Visit **www.garnethill.com** and search for "organic cotton towels." Selections of soft, extra-thirsty, bathsheet-size towels are great beach choices.

Organic Finger Play

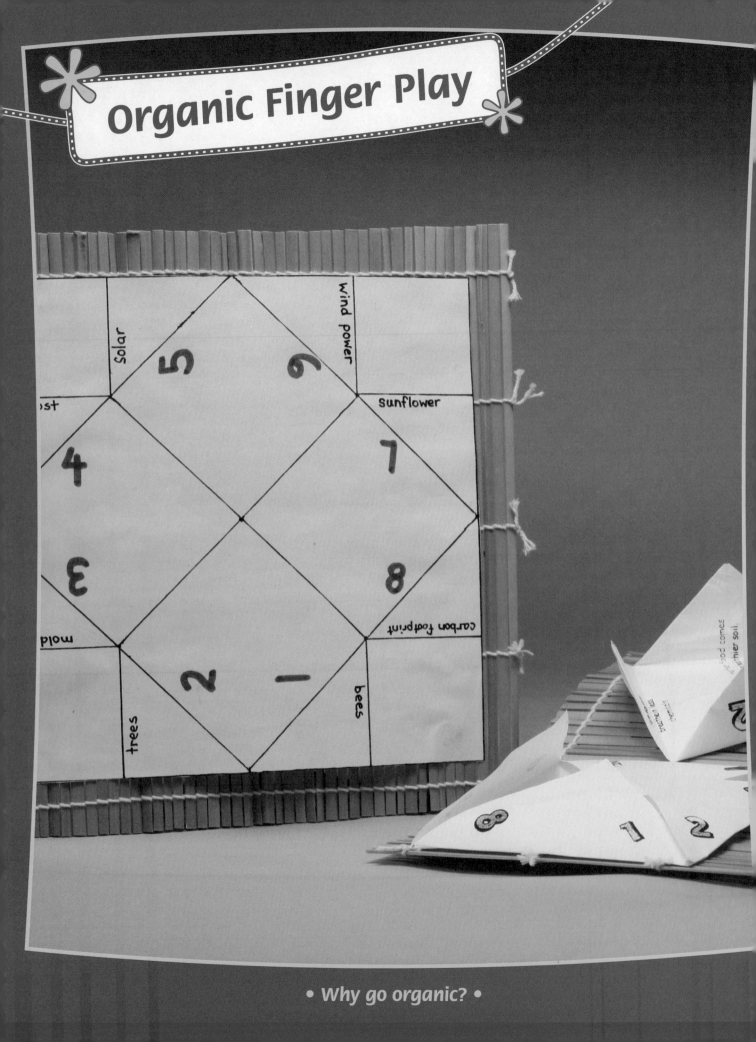

Materials

Paper squares, ranging in size from 4" square (25cm²) to 7" square (45cm²)
Markers

Directions

1. Place a dot in the center of each square.
2. Fold the four corner points into the center dot, creasing the fold into place.
3. Flip over the square and repeat by bringing the four corner points into the center dot, creasing the fold into place.
4. Fold this new, smaller folded square in half in one direction and crease the fold.
5. Unfold and fold in half in the other direction to make fold lines for both directions.
6. Put your thumb and index finger of each hand under the corner flaps.

Chat Point

Each flap is a Chat Point and a reason to seek out your local organic offerings.

Mini-Chat Point

Organic fruits and veggies are Mother Nature's gift to your body.

7. Squeeze your thumbs and fingers together to open and close.
8. Once all your fold lines are firm, open it up to hand-print in the words and numbers.
9. Write in the reasons to go organic from the list below on the innermost folds:
   • Organic farming helps protect our water supply.
   • Kids ingest more chemicals than adults do.
   • Farm workers breathe in fewer toxins.
   • Healthier food comes from healthier soil.
   • Buying organic supports small family farms.
   • Organic = less chemicals on earth.
   • Pesticide is not a condiment.
   • More vitamins and minerals.
10. Add numbers as shown in the photograph or replace the numbering system with different green words like: wind power, bees, bamboo and reusable.
11. Color the outside squares where your thumb and index finger will go in different shades of green.

How to Play

1. With thumbs and fingers holding the square, ask a friend to pick a color.
2. Spell out the color by opening and closing until you reach the end of the color word.
3. Keeping this section open, have your friend choose a square with a green word or number on it.
4. Do the same as Step 2 by spelling out the word, opening and closing for each letter until you reach the end of the word.
5. At this point, ask your friend to choose one more green word, and this time, unfold the flap and read the reason to go organic.

Above and Beyond!

In the U.S., visit **www.usda.gov** and search for "organic certification." Discover what goes into regulating and protecting the consumer before a "green" sticker is granted. In Canada, check **www.ccof.org** and for the U.K. and beyond you will find information for organic standards at **www.ifoam.org**.

Coming Up Roses

• Beyond packing peanuts •

Materials

Container (such as bisphenol-a buster)
Dried rose petals
Essential oil (www.auracacia.com) *optional*

Directions

1. Whenever roses are received or when they are growing in the garden, pluck the petals off at the end of peak blooming. Save petals in a container to dry out. With permission, a friend or neighbor's garden may be perfect for collecting fallen petals.

2. If you wish to add scent, use one drop of essential oil for a handful of petals.

3. Add rose petals to gift boxes, envelopes and even the bathtub.

Chat Point

Gifting can be made beautiful without bows and ribbons. Rose petals are in relative abundance so keep the collection going and you will always have an addition for your special packages and envelopes. Small candy-coated chocolates such as the Chocolate Sunflower Seed Drops pictured, take colorful, edible packaging to a new level.

Mini-Chat Point

Picking flowers is fun, but adults usually only allow picking of weed flowers. Enjoy the so-called weeds too. Clover dries well and smells like honey.

Above and Beyond!

When possible, purchase fair trade roses. This will ensure that those working in the flower fields of origin are not exposed to dangerous levels of toxins in their daily work life. Seems only fair. For more information, visit www.transfairusa.org.

Materials

Old maps
Cardboard
Scissors
Single-hole punch
Old shoelaces
Glue

Directions

1. Cut out countries, states, provinces or lakes of interest.

2. Glue onto cardboard and cut around the outlines of each one.

3. Using the single-hole punch, space out holes around the outline.

4. Thread shoelaces in and out or make a pattern stitch around the outline of the sewing card.

Chat Point

With the GPS (global positioning service) taking over our navigational skills, the glove compartment foldable map is becoming a thing of the past. Instead of tossing them, reuse them by making this set of sewing cards into a gift.

Mini-Chat Point

Find a printed map of your town and make a gift set for a friend. Save a map!

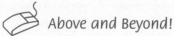 Above and Beyond!

While printed topographical and hiking trail maps still make perfect sense for outdoor adventure, it is great to be rid of the excessive foldable maps that take up space in rest stops and glove compartments alike. For a solar-powered GPS unit, check out **www.ubergizmo.com** and search for "ftech solar GPS."

Denim Do-Over

• Bisphenol-a buster •

Materials

1 bisphenol-a water bottle
1 pair of old denim jeans
Scissors
Pen
Hot glue gun

Directions

1. Plug in hot glue gun to preheat.

2. Cut out seam from one denim leg, cutting close to stitching line on both sides.

3. Cut entire fabric leg off from remaining jean material.

4. To measure amount of denim required to cover bottle, place lid-free bottle on its side on top of denim fabric leg.

5. Mark a starting point with a pen, and roll bottle forward allowing an extra 2" (51mm) before marking the finishing point.

6. Allow ½" (13mm) on the top and bottom and mark accordingly, joining up with the other marks to form a rectangle.

7. Cut rectangle out of denim fabric.

8. Using hot glue gun, make a straight line across bottom of water bottle and stick on both open, cut ends of seam to meet in the middle.

9. Have both strap sides fit snugly up the sides of the bottle, gluing in place, forming an over-the-shoulder length strap.

10. Length of strap may be shortened by double knotting seam at any point.

11. Finish with hot glue gun covering whole surface of bottle except where lid will screw back on.

12. Working quickly, roll water bottle on denim, gathering and gluing extra fabric on the bottom over the exposed seam.

Chat Point

Instead of sending your unhealthy, non-biodegradable, chemical-laced bottle to the landfill, use it to collect or store things that are not food related. Use it for keys, ID and money.

Mini-Chat Point

Since water bottles should never have been made with a chemical that leaches into your water in the first place, use the bottle mistake for something else, just not food or drink. Collect shells, pennies and buttons, take stuff to day camp in it...anything but water.

Above and Beyond!

The über-reusable water bottles at **www.sigg.com** come in refreshing graphics that work for picnics and in the executive office.

Green Day

By Hannah Rosenoff

Poor, poor polar bear
None of this is truly fair

We melt their ice and hungry they go
This day is here to help them so

Put on an organic shirt
'Cause lots of animals are getting hurt

Use a Sigg bottle to help out
Don't waste water from your sprinkler spout

Ecopaper, ideal bite
This is our chance to fight, fight, fight!

Materials

Handful of broken golf tees from your local enthusiast or golf course

One tired picture frame from a bottom drawer or dusty basement shelf

Hot glue gun

Directions

1. Plug in hot glue gun to preheat.

2. Clean picture frame and lay flat on work surface.

3. Arrange golf tees in desired fashion to cover the frame.

4. Secure individual tees with hot glue gun.

5. Write or draw a sustainable message, poem or cartoon to place in picture frame.

6. Give to your favorite golfer or mini-golfer.

Chat Point

What are you teed off at? Perhaps plastic shopping bags that continue to rear their ugly heads in malls and grocery stores? In addition to getting into the habit of bringing reusable bags into grocery stores AND the mall, start a conversation for change with the grocery store, drug store, clothing store, etc. Find out who to write to and do your part to take the plastic bag one more step towards extinction.

Mini-Chat Point

We have way too many plastic bags. They become litter in our streams, rivers and oceans sometimes causing sea creatures to eat little bits of them...major stomachache or worse.

Above and Beyond!

Since plastic bags are derived from petroleum, their eventual elimination is necessary when we have other options. Biodegradable bags of all sorts are being developed, and while the jury is still out, keep an eye out for them. In the meantime, drop in at **www.plasticbageconomics.com** and remember to continue using your reusable bags.

Good Friends Come to the Back Door

• Getting twiggy with it •

Materials

Thin sticks of varying lengths, willow
  or forsythia are pliable and work well
Assortment of dried flowers
Rubber bands

Directions

1. Plan a word to use like dream, explore, create, welcome, your name, etc.

2. Begin by breaking off sections of sticks to form the outline of the letters.

3. Arrange in sequence.

4. Using rubber bands, secure the ends by wrapping around several times until desired stick direction is reached to form letters.

5. Place dried flowers near natural connections of the letter sticks, using existing rubber bands or adding new ones.

6. Prop letters against a wall, place on a mantle or hang individual letters by their top rubber bands.

Chat Point

Plastic and PVC decorations have taken over our yards and doors. They may be colorful, but there is an army of retired inflatable pumpkins and plastic snowmen in a landfill near you.

Mini-Chat Point

Where do all the decorations go when their job is done or we get tired of them? Make decorations that can go in your composter afterward. You will amaze yourself.

Above and Beyond!

Before being swept into the 50-percent-off post-holiday decoration bonanza, consider alternative decorations for the next holiday. Borrow a bunny from your local farm for an Easter visit to your house. Make a pine-cone wreath. Bake alphabet cookie shapes into a holiday greeting word. Save hole-punch holes in a special container to use as confetti for a birthday. Visit **www.ecobites.com** and search for "party decorations" for more festive ideas.

Materials

1 empty, rinsed gallon (4L) milk jug
Pull ties from the tops of two milk jugs
Single-hole punch
Scissors
Drinking glass
Pencil
Photo collection with one portrait shot for the cover

Directions

1. Select two of the flattest sides of the milk jug and cut out both in a rectangular shape.

2. Shape the rectangles by cutting according to the lines pre-existing on the milk jug or leave in a rectangular shape.

3. Stack photo collection, leaving the front portrait shot for a cut-out window.

4. Trace the bottom of a drinking glass on the milk jug front, lining it up with an appropriate picture subject to be displayed through the cut-out window.

5. Carefully, cut out the circle (sometimes easier by poking a scissor hole into the middle of the plastic first before cutting out to the edge of the circle).

6. Punch two holes in the top of the photo collection.

7. Line up the milk jug front and back cover and punch holes in them as well.

8. Thread pull ties from milk jugs through all holes to hold photo book together.

Reduce, Reuse and Recycle

Chat Point

While reducing packaging on many consumer products, it is most difficult to get milk any other way than in a large container. Before sending your weekly milk jug to overcrowded landfills, incurring transportation fees along the way, find other uses as much as possible. Clean and store the bottom halves and use to give away plants or present gifts.

Mini-Chat Point

With your next empty milk jug, cut out the top spout until it fits snugly onto your head. Decorate as an astronaut helmet and you've saved another milk jug from the dump.

 Above and Beyond!

Write or email your local officials about specific milk container recycling and send them the link to **www.milkcontainerrecycling.com** where cost-effective measures are already humming along.

Hypoallergenic Bouquet

• Paper or plastic? Neither! •

Materials

Plastic goodie bags, dental supply bags, other small
bags that refuse to go away
12" (30cm) sticks
Garbage bag or gift bag twist-ties
Dry vase

Directions

1. Fold plastic bags in a fan pattern.

2. Cut rounded edges on both ends to form petals.

3. Holding the fan pattern in place, secure a twist-tie tightly around the middle.

4. Fluff out the petals to form a flower.

5. For thicker flowers, fold more than one plastic bag in the fan pattern before tying all together.

6. Use ends of same twist-tie to fasten to the end of a stick.

7. Display in dry vase of any kind.

Chat Point

When choosing party favors, give a reusable shopping bag even though it is quite large compared to the mini-plastic goodie bags. They are attractive and necessary to change the paper or plastic habits in the grocery stores and malls. For small giveaways at the doctor or dentist, say "no thank you" to the plastic bags and soon they will be a thing of the past as well.

Mini-Chat Point

Remind adults around you to grab the reusable bag whenever you unclick your seat belt to go into a food, clothes or pet store, so another plastic bag doesn't come back into your life.

Above and Beyond!

Check out www.greenfeet.net and in the Looking for an Article? box, choose view alphabetically and find the article entitled, "Paper vs. Plastic — The Shopping Bag Debate."

Longest Playing Record

• *Strains of salty and sweet* •

Materials

2 old vinyl long-playing records ("LP") and 45 sizes
 from basement, grandma's attic or garage sale
Large cardboard box
Pencil
Scissors
Hot glue gun

Directions

1. Plug in hot glue gun to preheat.

2. Plan on making two snack trays with the long-playing records and as many coasters as you have 45s.

3. On the cardboard, trace around the LPs and cut out cardboard circle with scissors.

4. Do the same for the coasters.

5. Using the hot glue gun, secure the LPs and the 45s to the cardboard outlines.

6. Place snack bowls on tray, pass out the drinks and coasters and you can "Cut Footloose."

Chat Point

Starve a landfill by rescuing interesting things like LPs and 45s to give them another life. They are durable, collectible, most often free and lead to a vintage conversation.

Mini-Chat Point

Don't the LPs and 45s look strong? They would just take up space in a landfill so it is much better to turn them into something else. Look at your garbage before it heads into the garbage truck. Is there anything someone else can use? Is there another creative use for it?

Above and Beyond!

If Tupperware® can be made into a cool-looking dress, the sky is the limit as to what we can do with our so-called trash. Visit **www.lianakabel.com**, click on Designs and then scroll down further to another Design link. As you scroll, you will see fantastic plastic creations.

Paper Trail

• *Glossy rescue* •

Materials

2 mail-order catalogs or calendars
1 colorful cardboard cereal box
Hot glue gun
Scissors

Directions

1. Plug in hot glue gun to preheat.

2. Open catalogs to central pages.

3. Remove and recycle several pages until you have five or six layers remaining.

4. Turn over the opened catalogs and select a favorite cover catalog to be facing you with its cover page.

5. Cut through from the bottom end to within 1" (25mm) of the top end, making fringes of 1" (25mm) in width all along the catalog or calendar.

6. Place the second catalog or calendar, open-faced and sideways, on the left of the first one.

7. Cut in the same manner, from bottom to top, without cutting all the way through.

8. Begin weaving from left to right, gluing each strip to the end piece on the right.

9. Continue until completed, cutting off any excess lengths on either end.

10. Cut a frame out of a cereal box and glue around the edges to tidy up the place mat.

Chat Point

Even once you have eliminated most unwanted junk mail, there are still catalogs and calendars that can enjoy another life. Put them to use for a week, a month or longer as eclectic place mats that will inspire sustainable dinner conversations.

Mini-Chat Point

When you finish reading your favorite kids' magazine, pass it on to a friend. Calendar pictures are great to weave into mixed-up pictures as a place mat.

Above and Beyond!

Use www.41pounds.org as the all-around service to stop junk mail in the U.S. www.stopjunkmail.ca handles Canadian junk and www.stopjunkmail.org.uk addresses the problem in the U.K. Write regular emails to your favorite magazines to stop "magazine fallout" — all those annoying papers that fall on the ground when you open their publication and meet their hasty end, unread, in the trash can.

Putting Up the Memories

• A jarring vacation •

Materials

Small trip souvenir items such as:
- Ticket stubs
- Napkin logos
- Native sand, rocks or shells
- Stickers
- Tiny souvenir items of interest
- Cleaned jam jars
- Hot glue gun

Directions

1. Plug in hot glue gun to preheat.

2. Plan a scene or summary of your trip by sorting out your trinkets.

3. Determine what would look best in the jar facing front and center.

4. Begin by placing sand, rocks or shells in the bottom of the jar.

5. Add items of interest by gluing or setting in place to make it visually appealing from the front.

6. If desired, use ribbon, string or fabric to cover the lid as well.

7. Add a mini-LED flashlight for accent lighting in the event of company who may view your mantle display of long weekends and vacations.

Chat Point

Knowing that souvenirs have to fit in a jar already reduces the plastic element of souvenirs. Focusing on native sand, rocks or shells make for research opportunities to learn more about the area. It is fun to spill them out too and look at it all over again. Destination T-shirts are generally worn right after vacation and often, never again.

Mini-Chat Point

Collect ice-cream napkin logos, feathers and anything that fits in a jar to help you remember the good times of a long weekend or vacation. There will always be pictures for the rest of the memories.

Above and Beyond!

Reusing jam jars is a beautiful recycling moment. To see recycled glass in affordable art and useful forms, visit artist Stephen Kitras at **www.kitras.com**. Purchase through **www.uncommongoods.com**.

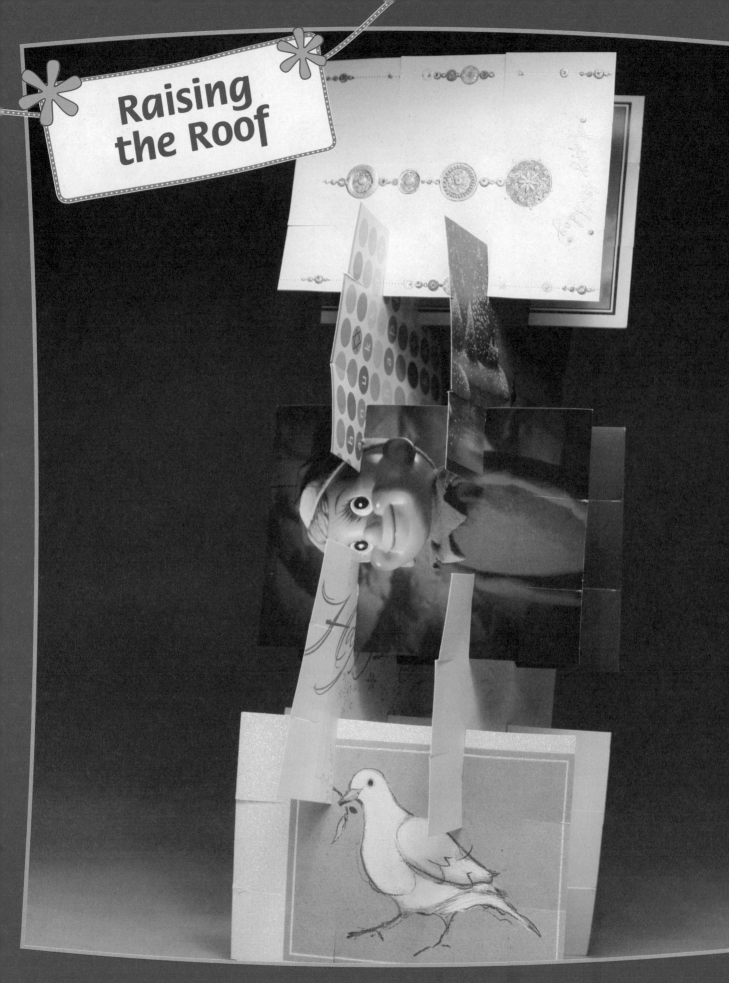

Raising the Roof

Materials

20 recycled birthday or holiday cards of rectangular
  shape (or worn-out playing cards)
Scissors

Directions

1. On the long side of the rectangles, cut two even slits on each side.

2. Cut one slit on each end of the short side of the rectangles.

3. Connect the cards in any building and design form.

4. Add more cards to the collection and build a city of your imagination.

Chat Point

Extend the joy of cards by giving them another life before they go into the recycling bin. When buying your next greeting, look for those printed on recycled paper before felling more trees for the fleeting good wishes.

Mini-Chat Point

To make cards, it takes BILLIONS of trees every year. Send one on the computer instead.

Above and Beyond!

From www.ekoni.com comes the option to send eye-catching sentiments and they'll plant a tree every time you do. U.K. based, worldwide reach, and saving trees one card at a time.

Materials

Used wine corks
Old buttons
Hot glue gun
Once-used tissue paper
Ink pad

Directions

1. Plug in hot glue gun to preheat.

2. Set aside buttons that have interesting, flat faces.

3. Glue one button onto each cork.

4. Flatten tissue paper.

5. Press button side onto ink pad and make prints on the tissue, rocking back and forth to make original designs and patterns.

Chat Point

Since cork wine-stoppers are as natural as can be, sourced from the bark of the cork oak tree, they can be tossed into the compost pile — the ultimate free recycling plan.

Mini-Chat Point

There are millions and millions of wine corks in the world. Save them and make something interesting out of them. Otherwise, seagulls will just peck at them in landfills.

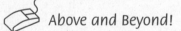 **Above and Beyond!**

Visit **www.recorkamerica.com** to see if there is a U.S. location near you that collects used wine corks. Or you can collect them yourself from friends and family and mail them in to their warehouse. They also list other cork collection sites to help you find a more convenient drop off location.

Upcycled Power Ties

Materials

7 to 8 neckties that men in your life no longer enjoy
Measuring tape
Marker
Scissors
Twine

Directions

1. Select two ties to be straps and set aside.

2. On a flat surface, arrange ties facedown in opposite directions, alternating the directions of the wider portions to form front of top.

3. With ties outstretched, focus on the center of the top, aligning the ties.

4. Using scissors, make small cuts in the ties from top to bottom, and 2" (5cm) apart from side to side on the front section of the top only.

5. Cut 6" (15cm) lengths of twine, making them easy to work with, and thread them through the holes, joining up sections of neighboring ties.

6. Tie in double knots.

7. Keeping ties facedown, place the two strap ties in position with the front of the top.

8. Cut a small hole and knot in place.

9. Carefully turn over the tie top.

10. Measure the chest of the individual who will wear the top to determine the length of wrap-around ties, and how long the top should extend with straps measured to size.

11. Using a marker, write the measurements on the back of the ties.

12. Cut the ties intended to function as straps, allowing an extra 1" (25mm) for overlapping.

13. Using twine, knot the straps in place as suited to the individual wearer.

14. Remaining back ties may be layered, cut holes at 2" (5cm) intervals and knot in place.

15. Wear with snug-fitting underlayer and you'll make quite a fashion statement of upcycling.

Chat Point

Some things go out of fashion but are structurally in perfect condition. Reinvent your wardrobe before returning to the mall.

Mini-Chat Point

You know about recycling, and now you have a new word — upcycling. It's taking something headed for the garbage and turning it into something new. Introduce your school to **www.terracycle.net** where drink pouches, cookie wrappers and energy bar wrappers are multi-purposing into other forms.

Above and Beyond!

Visit **www.sustainablog.org** and conduct a search for "upcycling projects" to find a wallet made from an inner tube, a chair crafted out of election campaign signs and much more.

Build Your Own Wind Farm

Materials

Paper squares from greatly appreciated artwork
  before it reaches the recycling bin
Hot glue gun
Scissors
Paper clips, in same amount as number of squares
Sticks of varying lengths, in same amount as number
  of squares
(If sticks are unavailable, you can achieve the same
  with pencils.)

Directions

1. Plug in hot glue gun to preheat.

2. Draw a dot in the middle of each square.

3. Cut in a straight line from each corner of the square,
   leaving 1" (25mm) uncut before hitting the dot.

4. Curl one point down at a time to the center dot
   and glue in place, holding until secure.

5. Unbend the paper clips (you're allowed to).

6. Once glue is dry for all four points, poke a hole
   through the middle with one end of the paper clip.

7. Insert paper clip, creating a bendy or swirly center
   of the pinwheel on the front.

8. Wrap back end of paper clip around the top of a
   stick.

9. Make as many as you can and display in multiple
   vases.

Chat Point

Wind power is providing electricity to an increasing number of homes. Check with your local utility provider to see if you can participate in wind power as well. If you live on a larger property outside of suburbia, you can investigate installing your own mini-wind turbine.

Mini-Chat Point

Wind comes from so many different places. Experiment with some of your pinwheels by blowing on them, putting them in front of a fan and taking them outside. Even someone just running by will make it move. That's why wind is becoming a major power generator.

Above and Beyond!

Learn more about the alternative energy sourced by our very own stiff breezes by visiting **www.powerhousekids.com** and search for "wind power."

Ghost Town

• Red berry, blueberry, blackberry •

Materials

1 produce carton
12" (30cm) decorative trim, lace or ribbon
Hot glue gun
Marker

Directions

1. Plug in hot glue gun to preheat.

2. Measure trim with a small amount of overlap to wrap around the edge of the produce carton.

3. Using marker, write a phrase such as "No more phantom overload," or "This family is unplugged."

4. Spread a layer of glue around the entire perimeter of the produce carton and affix the trim.

5. Add cell phones and personal digital assistants to remain in their new holding bin until charging becomes necessary.

Chat Point

As with any habit, practicing makes it automatic. After your gadgets are charged, be sure to unplug them as they continue to draw electricity even when they look harmlessly idle.

Mini-Chat Point

When your body is finished sleeping and recharging for the next day, do you keep your head on your pillow past the morning wake-up time? No! You're energized and ready for action. It would be such a waste of a good morning to keep your head stuck on that pillow for the whole day.

Above and Beyond!

All manner of solar chargers are available now, so start the switch. Look into **www.solio.com** and discover that wherever there's a ray, the Solio® will be working for you.

Materials

Cardboard shoebox

Several digital photo prints, or computer printouts
  of a child in action poses such as kicking a soccer
  ball, at bat for baseball or softball, shooting a hockey
  puck, rollerblading, etc.

Hot glue gun

Scissors

4 sticks

Paper

Alternative Energy

Chat Point

Sample messages for your speak bubbles can
include: Clothes last longer washed in cold
water. No one ever said, "Look at their clothes!
They suffer from cold-water washing!"

Mini-Chat Point

When your dirty clothes go into the washing
machine, most of the energy needed to clean
those clothes is used up in heating the water.
Next time your family is doing laundry ask to
press the cold water button.

Directions

1. Plug in hot glue gun to preheat.

2. Lay cardboard box down flat so it will be easy to
   work with.

3. Cut around the outline of the child pictured,
   leaving out the ball, bat, stick, etc.

4. Think about a sustainable message you can
   represent with photos and extra materials from
   around the house.

5. Using scissors, make small slits in the sides, top or
   bottom of the shoebox to insert the sticks.

6. Glue photos onto sticks and add decorations.

7. Draw one or more speak bubbles to get your
   sustainable living message across.

8. Glue speak bubble to back of child's photo head.

9. Display prominently and discuss often.

 Above and Beyond!

www.seventhgeneration.com offers laundry detergents that really work in cold water and missing ingredients
include: allergens, phosphates, optical brighteners and chlorine bleach. The only thing you will see is the money
you saved on your electric bill.

Winter Fun Preservation

• Snowball fight •

Materials

Old knee-highs and/or pantyhose; runs in the hose are fine, but holes won't work

Small bag of flour (low-grade bulk in most grocery stores and very cheap, perfect for crafts)

Markers

Mittens

Scissors

Measuring cup

Directions

1. Cut off 8" (20cm) from knee-highs or pantyhose, measuring from the toes upward.

2. Scoop two cups (250g) of flour into each piece of hose.

3. Tie a tight double knot after settling the flour in the bottom of the hose.

4. With knot on top, give snowball a personality with any sort of face.

5. Grab your mittens and have a snowball fight, even if it's a hot, humid day.

6. Poofs of flour upon impact add to the fun factor.

Chat Point

Keep the snow in childhood. Who doesn't love a snowball fight? Snow is also the source for a lifetime sport if you become a snowboarder, skier or snow tuber. You can help keep the Arctic temperatures cool by using the smallest oven available to heat up or cook one-dish meals.

Mini-Chat Point

Did you ever switch on the oven light and see just one loaf of banana bread or zucchini bread in all that space? It bakes just as well in a convection oven and some toaster ovens. The mouthwatering smell remains the same.

Above and Beyond!

Take a look at **www.nrdc.org** to determine if a membership is right for you. Their online action network gives you a voice on global warming issues and makes it easy to send emails to decision-making officials with factual positions.

Materials

8 glass baby food jars with lids, cleaned and dry
8 colors from the Color Key, page 7
Stick

Directions

1. Make all colors listed in the Color Key on page 7.

2. Pour one color into each of the eight glasses.

3. Create an order from lowest water level to highest water level to achieve different tonality for each jar.

4. Using stick, play notes in succession and make up your own tunes.

Chat Point

Colors can be derived from many natural sources such as fruits, herbs, flower petals and plants. Using them to color eggs and fabrics keeps synthetic dyes out of our water table and drinking sources.

Mini-Chat Point

Native peoples from around the world have always used nature's dyes to make their lives more colorful. It's more fun to do it yourself too.

Above and Beyond!

Check out **www.reverbrock.org** and discover how Reverb educates musicians and fans alike to promote environmental sustainability. With so many partners listed, from Jack Johnson to Sheryl Crow, and so many more in between, concerts, musicians and fans are changing their wasteful ways one note at a time.

Cork Torque

• Too hot to handle •

Materials

5 corks saved from wine bottles
2 bamboo skewers

Directions

1. Break bamboo skewers in half.

2. Poke a skewer half into top end of one cork to a depth of ½" (13mm).

3. Repeat the same on bottom end of same cork.

4. Continuing with same cork, poke other two skewer halves into sides of cork to form a lower case "t" with the first skewer halves.

5. Place a cork on the ends of each of the "t" points, to a depth of ½" (13mm).

Chat Point

Cork-producing oak forests absorb carbon dioxide, house some endangered species and prevent soil erosion. The Forest Stewardship Council has been active in the cork-producing countries to maintain standards that allow for sustainable cork harvesting practices and the continuation of the livelihood it provides for many native peoples.

Mini-Chat Point

Did you know cork comes from an evergreen tree and is used to make shoe soles, flooring, handles, yoga mats, bulletin boards and more?

Above and Beyond!

Log on to **www.rainforest-alliance.org** and search for "put a sustainable cork in it" to find out why the trend towards synthetic wine stoppers is not a good one.

Oceans Of Fun

• See sea star swim strongly •

Materials

1 cup (221g) baking soda
½ cup (64g) corn starch
¾ cup (180ml) water
Small pot
Stirring utensil
Heat-resistant surface such as a countertop, cutting
  board, etc. to work on
Seaside Summer cookie cutters
  (www.kingarthurflour.com) or
  beach theme cookie cutters
Priti™ nail polish for unique decorating features
  (www.pritiorganicspa.com, search under
  Where to Buy for retailers in the U.K. and Canada)

Directions

1. Combine baking soda, cornstarch and water in a pot over low heat.

2. Stir steadily for four minutes until a mashed potato consistency is achieved.

3. Turn mixture onto heat-resistant surface to cool.

4. Start kneading and pressing dough into a smoother texture.

5. Flatten dough to ½" (13mm) thickness.

6. Using starfish and shell cookie cutters, press out a collection of sea shapes.

7. Air-dry for several hours or overnight before decorating.

8. For unique decorating details for shell patterns, starfish tentacles, etc., paint with Priti nail polishes free of toluene, formaldehyde and dibutyl phthalate.

Chat Point

Being aware that the balance of ocean life is delicate causes us to act more cautiously in our care of the ocean water. When the ocean is not healthy, some populations surge and others wane. Predators of the starfish are large fish and sharks. If there are not enough predators, the starfish population gets out of control, as it has done in some ocean coral areas where it strips coral clean, causing it to die.

Mini-Chat Point

Scientists don't call them starfish anymore. Now, the term is "sea star" because they really are not fish at all. They are known for the amazing fact that if a predator snatches off one arm, the sea star will grow back another one in its place.

Above and Beyond!

Peek at Google Earth's **www.protectplanetocean.org**. It is a tool that helps non-profits develop online maps and gives researchers a place to show their findings from all corners of the world.

Show Some Mussel

• Flex your mussels •

Materials

1 tired wreath from your garage, basement, attic
30 sustainably harvested mussels (approximation allowing for breakage and different wreath sizing)
30 small beads (approximation based on number of mussels used)
Hot glue gun

Directions

1. Plug in hot glue gun to preheat.

2. Follow directions for steaming and enjoying a large mussel appetizer.

3. Save shells and clean them.

4. Gently break in half and separate into a "left shell" pile and a "right shell" pile.

5. Choosing either all lefties or righties, arrange in succession around the old wreath and secure individual shells with hot glue gun.

6. Add a decorative accent by adding small beads at the base of the mussel shells with hot glue gun.

Chat Point

Mussels, oysters and clams are known for their amazing filtering abilities. They are being put to work in our waterways, successfully handling algae blooms and many heavy metals by filtering gallons and gallons into purified water.

Mini-Chat Point

Hold a mussel, clam or oyster shell in your hand and pour a whole gallon of water over it. When that mussel, clam or oyster was alive, it would clean many, many gallons of water in one day as the water passed through it's shells. Wow!

Above and Beyond!

For a fascinating peek at mussels in action, visit **www.gulfofmaine.org**, click on Gulfwatch and find out about mussel biomonitoring.

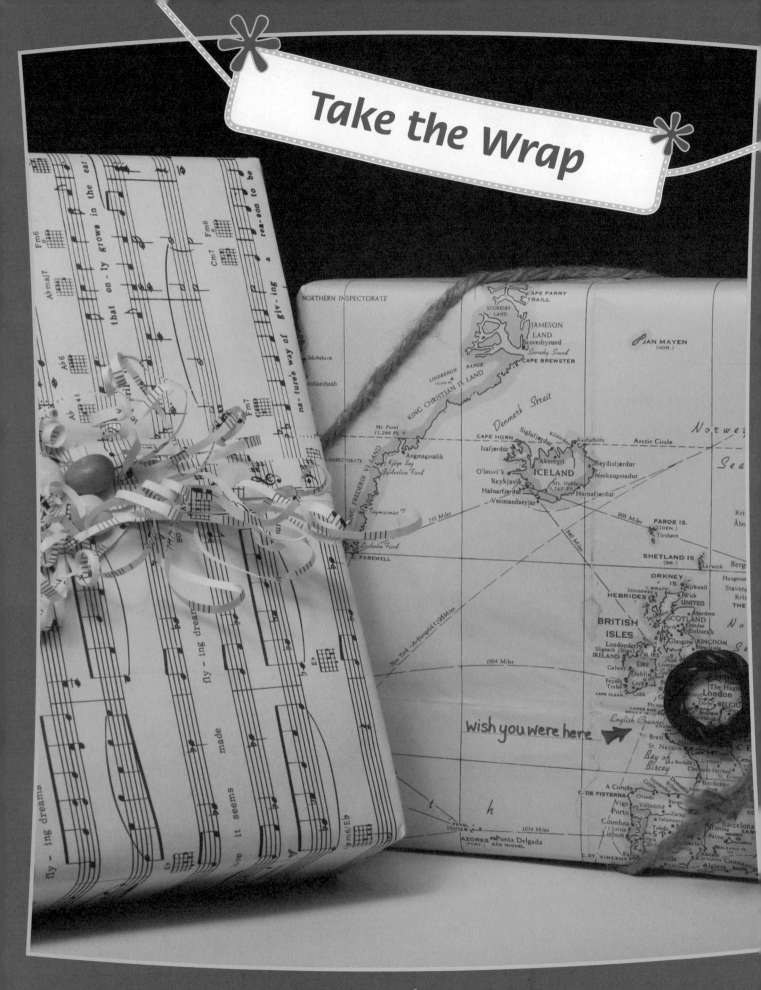

Take the Wrap

Materials

Old programs from performances and events
Old travel brochures
Old sheet music
Old maps
Bags of SunDrops (or similar chocolate drops)
Packages of candy licorice vines
Scissors
Tape

Directions

1. Set aside a space to save interesting papers for wrapping occasions.

2. When wrapping a gift, include a bag of SunDrops or licorice vines and reserve a bag for self-indulgence, gluing on one or two for a unique package decoration.

Chat Point

While the trend is to go paperless in corporations and institutions, some glossy prints are still here. Put them to work, after enjoying them, in the useful role of saving other trees from the wrapping-paper frenzy.

Mini-Chat Point

Your homemade wrapping paper is more fun for you to make and give than just pulling out another piece of flowery, swirly, striped, glittery wrapping paper made in a factory.

Above and Beyond!

Check out **www.veganessentials.com** and search for "Candy Tree organic licorice vines." For chocolate or peanut SunDrops, visit **www.sunspire.com**.

Basket Weaving 101

• Sticks for kicks •

Materials

Armful of willow or forsythia twigs pruned from a tree
Twist-ties from bread or rubber bands
1 rectangular brick or other heavy object of similar
 size
Packing tape
Dried flowers, fallen bark
Paper square
Hole punch
12" (30cm) twine

Directions

1. Lay about 10 twigs next to each other in a row
   keeping one end even.

2. Tape even end of twigs securely in place on a flat
   surface.

3. Weave another set of about 10 twigs in and out
   of the taped down set of twigs to form a loosely
   woven center square.

4. Lay brick on woven square to weigh down bottom.

5. Use additional twigs to weave around and around
   until desired height is reached.

6. Form a simple handle and use twine to knot in
   place.

7. Embellish with dried flowers or fallen bark.

8. Write a paper tag, punch a hole in it and tie it with
   twine to your basket indicating who created this
   special basket and pass it on.

Chat Point

There are plenty of sustainable baskets available for sale, but they hail from thousands of miles away. Try your hand at making some from local tree pruning, tall grasses or pine-needle branches.

Mini-Chat Point

Put a green habit changer in your basket and give it to a special friend. Give them a reusable water bottle, a bamboo bowl or a shower timer and help jump-start a friend into sustainable living habits too…we're all in this together.

Above and Beyond!

If pruning is not your thing, visit **www.btcelements.com** and conduct a search for "potato chip trash basket."

Making Mud Pies

• Don't cave in •

Materials

Straw from your local farm, garden nursery or craft store

Dirt from your backyard or potting soil from your garden nursery

Tub or pail for mixing

Several thick sticks for stirring

Thick cardboard box broken down into a platform

Stone surface

Directions

1. Wear old, washable clothing so you can dig in without inhibition.

2. In the tub or pail, mix a measure of dirt with one-half measure of water.

3. Stir with the stick until a pasty consistency has been achieved, adding water if necessary.

4. Add in handfuls of straw until the mixture starts to hold together.

5. Using a cardboard base area, bring handfuls of the mud and straw onto the cardboard.

6. Using your best sculptural skills, shape a mound.

7. With your fist, make an indentation to form a cave-like shape.

8. Set to dry in the sun or on a table in your home.

Chat Point

You just made one of the primary primitive dwellings known to humans. Picture it set back against a mountain with maximum sunlight exposure. These shelters provided warmth and protection from the elements in the winter and shade in the summer with cool walls from overnight drops in temperature. It was the original LEED-certified home. Think of one way you can make your home more efficient. Add a rain barrel for retrieving water that can be added to the landscape, a solar hot water heater or sustainable flooring like bamboo or a wood native to your area.

Mini-Chat Point

Check your bedroom and see if you have really old carpet or a floor that's had more mileage than your parents' frequent flier cards. Maybe it's time to replace it with bamboo flooring. Besides being breakfast, lunch and dinner for the panda bear, some bamboo varieties can grow more than a foot (30cm) a day, which means there's a lot of bamboo around, making it a good choice for flooring.

Above and Beyond!

Check out the real meaning of LEED certified at www.greenhomeguide.org and www.usgbc.org. Find ways you can lower your utility bills and take one more step toward sustainable living by making some changes at home. For the ultimate LEED-certified building, visit the greenest museum at www.calacademy.org.

Passport to the World of Sustainable Living Habits

• No more fossil fools •

Materials

1 empty tea box package (**www.yogitea.com** houses
 fabulous tea offerings in artfully designed boxes)
Markers or crayons
Paper
Stapler
Scissors
Hole punch
2 small ribbon pieces

Directions

1. Break down a tea box and invert to make it inside
 out.

2. Measure one of the box sides to size paper.

3. Transfer measurements to paper and cut a supply
 of 16 papers.

4. Working on the colorful graphic side of the same
 box side that was measured, staple papers in place
 on top portion to allow for flipping.

5. Decorate cover to look official.

6. Keep a log of things you have changed in your
 house, someone else's life or at school on the path
 to sustainable living.

Chat Point

☐ Did you vacuum your refrigerator's coils?
☐ Have you eaten lower on the food chain
 for most of the week?
☐ Does your friend know about the bakery
 selling organic goodies, their store walls
 made of wheat, their cups made of corn, a
 discount if you come on bike or foot and
 the same front door since 1937?

Mini-Chat Point

There is a world of habit changing going on and
you are a part of it. Grab your wind-up flashlight
and go exploring. The new wind-up toys are
actually crank flashlights and radios working to
keep batteries out of hazardous waste. Check
into **www.earthtechproducts.com** for wind-up
fun that always works in a blackout.

Above and Beyond!

Visit **www.birdbathbakery.com**, as described in the Chat Point, and experience a new level of organic and
sustainable bakery.

Pointillism

Materials

Three-hole punch and single-hole punch with a
  buildup of holes in the catchall
Canvas or piece of paper to be inserted into frame
Old photos
Imagination
Pencil
Glue

Directions

1. Plan a picture as simple as a flower or as
   complicated as a meaningful scene to display a
   green message of sustainability and outline in
   pencil.

2. Empty hole punches onto work surface.

3. Cover pencil outline with glue.

4. As with the art form of pointillism, start placing the
   small dots in succession to cover pencil outline,
   forming a bigger picture.

Chat Point

Use dots to picture something as simple as
washing clothes in cold water or as complex
as not supporting genetically modified
crops that can land unbeknown to us in our
shopping carts.

Mini-Chat Point

Something as tiny as a hole-punch dot
becomes part of something much larger,
creating a picture. As small as your green
actions may be, they become part of the
bigger move in the right direction.

 Above and Beyond!

Click out this site, **www.green.cbc.ca** to get an idea for where a habit may be improved to sustainable status.

Toxic Emotions

jealous

excite

concern

lonely

worrie

surprised

• Balled up anger •

Materials

20 plastic bags from someone (even yourself) who
   pledged to give them up
Several lengths of string, twine or ribbon
Small strips of paper if handwriting or computer
   paper if printing
Pencil
Crayon
Marker
Scissors
Music

Directions

1. Print or handwrite some unhappy emotions that
   we all experience such as hurt, sad, fearful, jealous,
   nervous.

2. Add in a few pleasant emotions as well, such as
   giddy, happy, excited.

3. Place a plastic bag inside another and compact.

4. Repeat until all plastic bags have been used and
   you reach an approximate ball size of 6" (15cm)
   circumference.

5. Tie with several lengths of string, twine or ribbon to
   secure the ball shape.

6. Under the string, twine or ribbon, tuck in slips of
   the paper emotions.

7. To play, turn the music on while two or more
   players toss the ball around.

8. When the music stops, whoever is holding the
   ball picks out a paper emotion and tells about a
   moment when that emotion was felt and how it
   was handled.

9. Continue until all papers are removed.

Chat Point

The Toxic Emotions ball is an open forum
for kids and adults to express themselves.
As with pesticides and pollution, negative
emotions can be harmful as well. Utilizing the
remaining plastic bags in yours or a friend's
collection is a great way to toss out the
negative impact they pose.

Mini-Chat Point

Kids in some countries cannot afford to buy
a real soccer ball and make do with plastic
bags all tied together to kick around.

Above and Beyond!

Taking pollution a step further than the pesky plastic bag, visit **www.blacksmithinstitute.org** and find the "Top 10
World's Worst Pollution Problems."

The Studio Gallery
COMPLETION CHART
(craft projects)

Sunflower power
not a bit dour
a bee-welcoming tower
now it's your hour
take all that is sour
turn it into sustainable power!

Color or note each petal as you complete each project

Photo Guide List

No petroleum-based lipsticks or other enhancement cosmetics were harmed in the photography process. Photo composition and staging accessories were sourced from in-house inventory of recycling, crafts and decorative materials. If not noted below, items are no longer available. All produce, unless otherwise noted, came from Whole Foods Market®.

Apron Strings
• Honest Kids Berry Berry Lemonade and Tropical Tango Punch from www.honesttea.com.

Chocolate Orange Pudding
• Organic chocolate pudding from www.oetker.com.

Chili Ristra
• Organic fair trade cocoa powder from www.greenandblacks.com.

Cleans Up Nicely
• Van Saun Brook, River Edge, NJ.

Coconut Macaroons
• Organic shredded coconut from Let's Do…Organic® www.edwardandsons.com.

Coming Up Roses
• Chocolate sunflower seed drops from www.traderjoes.com.

Cork Torque
• Assorted corks; one from Pircas Negras Cabernet Sauvignon (Vegan) 2007, www.organicvintners.com.

Cover Photo
• www.shutterstock.com

Delegation of Pest Control Duties
• Pesticide-free zone yard sign, www.shopbeyondpesticides.org.

Epidermis Squirmis
• Coconut oil from www.spectrumorganics.com.

Express Yourself
• River Edge, NJ Green Day poem by Hannah Rosenoff printed on banana paper from www.ecopaper.com; polar bear notecard from www.edf.org.

Fair Trade Organic Chocolate Coffee Cake
• Maya Gold from www.greenandblacks.com.

From Darkness Comes Light
• Dark organic 85% chocolate bar from www.greenandblacks.com.
• Wild rice from www.lundberg.com.
• Organic raw pepitas, asparagus, mushrooms and zucchini from www.wholefoodsmarket.com.

Got Milk?
• Katrina Rosenoff

Happy Birthday Planet Earth
• Beeswax hand-rolled candles and beeswax sheets from www.magiccabin.com.

Home Invasion
• Japanese honeysuckle from River Edge, NJ.

Identity Theft
• Maple, gingko, oak, white pine, sweet gum from River Edge, NJ.

Invite Some Worms to Dinner
• Organic echinacea elder herbal tea bag from
  www.traditionalmedicinals.com.

It is My Beeswax
• Beeswax sheets from www.magiccabin.com.

Label Conscious
• "I love organics" from www.imorganic.com.
• "Bummer" from www.greenlabel.com.
• "Earth…I call it home" from T.h.e. Naturals through
  www.organiclifestyle.ca.

Making Mud Pies
• Kathe Kruse blue Nicki baby from
  www.kathe-kruse.com, available through
  www.willowtreetoys.com.

Monkey Business Trail Mix
• Preserve® tumbler from www.recycline.com.

Musically Inclined
• Earth's Best® baby food jars from
  www.earthsbest.com.

No More Plastic Smiles
• Carrot cake mix from
  www.simplyorganicfoods.com.
• Decorating sugars from www.indiatree.com.

Not the Only Pebble on the Beach
• Fruitabü™ Organic Smooshed™ Strawberry Flat from
  www.fruitabü.com.
• Beach-goers from Kashi Mighty Bites www.kashi.com.

Oceans of Fun
• Nail polish accents in Cornflower, Ballerina Peony
  and Fireglow from www.pritiorganicspa.com.

Paint the Town Green
• Baby food jars from www.earthsbest.com.

Paper Trail
• VivaTerra catalog from www.vivaterra.com.

Passport to World of Sustainable Living Habits
• Echinacea immune support tea box from
  www.yogitea.com.

Penny for Your Thoughts
• American penny, Canadian penny, British penny.

Picture Yourself
• Lola; Zachary Rosenoff as punter.

Pointillism
• Acanthus message board from
  www.ballarddesigns.com.
• Hannah Rosenoff.

Pollution Resolution
• Coconut oil from www.spectrumorganics.com.

Positive Reactions
• Dinner plate from www.treecycle.com.

Rice Pudding Comfort Food
• Preserve tumbler from www.recycline.com.

Send Your Soles
• Nike® Free running shoes from www.nike.com.

Solar Solutions
• Fruitabü Organic Smooshed Strawberry Flat from www.fruitabü.com.
• Golden Maple Leaf Delights hard candy from www.canadianmoose.com.

Speltapple Muffins
• Organic white spelt flour from 365™ Whole Foods Market™ Private Brand, www.wholefoodsmarket.com.

SunDrops Global Warming Bingo
• Chocolate SunDrops from www.sunspire.com.

Sunflower Gelato Cake
• Mango sorbetto and chocolate gelato from www.blackwellorganics.com.

Sweet Tooth
• Organic maple syrup from Trader Joe's®.
• Organic blue agave nectar from Wholesome® Sweeteners through www.organicsyrups.biz.

Take a Dive
• Monogrammed beach towels from www.garnethill.com.

Take Me Out to the Ballgame
• White and green bandana from Live Earth concert, 2007.

Take the Wrap
• Chocolate SunDrops from www.sunspire.com.
• Candy Tree organic licorice vines through www.veganessentials.com.

Toast of the Town
• Organic soft wheat bread from www.vermontbread.com.

Walking a Tightrope
• Bowl and plate from www.worldofgood.com by eBay®.

Your Neck of the Woods
• Tree stump in Lake Placid, NY.

Your Shoe Size
• Decorating sugars from www.indiatree.com.

Models
• Adam, Amar, Calvin, Colleen, Eiki, Emma, Hannah, Jared, Julian, Katrina, Miku, Montana, Noah, Patrick, Ryan, Sabrina, Shelby, Spencer, Trey, Veronica, Violet, William, and Zachary.

Additional Resources

www.askdrsears.com
www.GreenAmerica.com
www.greenteacher.com
www.earth911.com
www.emagazine.com
www.epicvancouver.com
www.gaiam.com
www.gogreenexpo.com
www.green.cbc.ca
www.greenhome.com
www.greenhomeguide.org
www.greenlivingonline.com
www.grist.org
www.HGTV.com - Danny Seo is the green guru.
www.idealbite.com
www.motherjones.com
www.nrdc.com
www.organicgardening.com
www.sierraclub.com
www.sustainlanegreenadnetwork.com
www.syracuseculturalworkers.com
www.thedailygreen.com
www.theecologist.com
www.utne.com
www.vivaterra.com
www.worldwildlife.com

Metric Table

LENGTH

Imperial Unit	Metric Unit
Inch	25.40 millimeters
Inch	2.54 centimeters
Foot	30.48 centimeters
Yard	0.91 meters
Mile	1.61 kilometers

Metric Unit	Imperial Unit
Millimeter	0.039 inches
Centimeter	0.39 inches
Meter	3.28 feet
Meter	1.09 yards
Kilometer	0.62 miles

AREA

Imperial Unit	Metric Unit
Square inch	6.45 square centimeters
Square foot	0.09 square meters
Square yard	0.84 square meters
Square mile	2.60 square kilometers
Cubic foot	0.028 cubic meters
Cubic yard	0.76 cubic meters
Acre	0.40 hectare

Metric Unit	Imperial Unit
Square centimeter	0.16 square inches
Square meter	1.20 square yard
Square kilometer	0.39 square miles
Cubic meter	35.23 cubic feet
Cubic meter	1.35 cubic yards
Hectare	2.47 acres

TEMPERATURE

Fahrenheit	Celsius
$°F = (°C \times 1.8) + 32$	$°C = (°F - 32) \div 1.8$
For example: $(20°C \times 1.8) + 32 = (36) + 32 = 68°F$	For example: $(68°F - 32) \div 1.8 = (36) \div 1.8 = 20°C$

WEIGHT (OR MASS)

Imperial Unit	Metric Unit
Ounce	28.35 grams
Pound	0.45 kilograms
UK ton (2240 pounds)	1.02 metric tons
US ton (2000 pounds)	0.91 metric tons

Metric Unit	Imperial Unit
Gram	0.035 ounces
Kilogram	2.21 pounds
Metric ton (1000kg)	0.98 UK tons
Metric ton (1000kg)	1.10 US tons

VOLUME

Imperial Unit	Metric Unit
Teaspoon (UK)	5.92 milliliters
Teaspoon (US)	4.93 milliliters
Tablespoon (UK)	17.76 milliliters
Tablespoon (US)	14.79 milliliters
Fluid ounce (UK)	28.41 milliliters
Fluid ounce (US)	29.57 milliliters
Pint (UK)	0.57 liters
Pint (US)	0.47 liters
Quart (UK)	1.14 liters
Quart (US)	0.95 liters
Gallon (UK)	4.55 liters
Gallon (US)	3.79 liters

Metric Unit	Imperial Unit
Milliliter	0.17 teaspoons (UK)
Milliliter	0.20 teaspoons (US)
10 Milliliter	0.56 tablespoons (UK)
10 Milliliter	0.68 tablespoons (US)
100 Milliliter	3.52 fluid ounces (UK)
100 Milliliter	3.38 fluid ounces (US)
Liter	1.76 pints (UK)
Liter	2.11 pints (US)
Liter	0.88 quarts (UK)
Liter	1.06 quarts (US)
Liter	0.22 gallon (UK)
Liter	0.26 gallon (US)

Index

About the Author

Wendy was born in Canada and has lived in Toronto, New York City, Atlanta and currently resides in River Edge, New Jersey. After the birth of her first child, Wendy became very aware of sustainable living choices. She started to take notice of how much "fake food" is consumed and it sparked her passion for organic foods. That interest and participation led her to pursue learning how to make earth-conscious, healthy living choices…and she's still a student.

As an active environmental enthusiast, Wendy enjoys spending time in schools and with Girl and Boy Scout groups sharing environmental-based projects. Inspired by kids of all grade levels who are willing to learn about new sustainable living habits they can employ, Wendy has found younger children's enthusiasm to be infectious when they burst with their own green living examples, while older children focus on the possibilities of what they can do in their family circle and outward.

This book is a natural extension of the food and craft classes Wendy initiated and conducted for young children at Whole Foods Market, Ridgewood, NJ. Wendy also co-chairs the Green Day event in River Edge, NJ and voluntarily promotes the movie, *Side Effects*, found in most stores or at **www.thekathleenshow.com**. Her Web site, **www.wendyrosenoff.com** provides monthly challenges under the Take Action heading.

Wendy graduated from The King's College in New York with a degree in business administration and economics and previously held key marketing, administration and executive positions in major manufacturing and banking sectors.

Wendy lives with her husband and three children in River Edge, NJ. She can be spotted around town wearing organic cotton, recycled rubber, water-based ink sneakers, toting a bag crocheted out of plastic bags and possibly rescuing a worm for her backyard composter.

Wendy is wearing a Power Fleece® of 55-percent hemp and 45-percent recycled plastic from **www.livity.org**

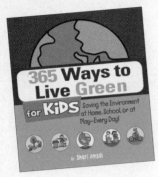